DIALOGUES ON DIVERSITY AND UNITY
IN FEDERAL COUNTRIES

A Global Dialogue on Federalism publications available

BOOK SERIES
Constitutional Origins, Structure, and Change in Federal Countries (2005), Volume 1
Distribution of Powers and Responsibilities in Federal Countries (2006), Volume 2
Legislative, Executive, and Judicial Governance in Federal Countries (2006), Volume 3
The Practice of Fiscal Federalism: Comparative Perspectives (2007), Volume 4
Foreign Relations in Federal Countries (2009), Volume 5

BOOKLET SERIES
Dialogues on Constitutional Origins, Structure, and Change in Federal Countries
(2005), Volume 1
Dialogues on Distribution of Powers and Responsibilities in Federal Countries (2005),
Volume 2
Dialogues on Legislative, Executive, and Judicial Governance in Federal Countries
(2006), Volume 3
Dialogues on the Practice of Fiscal Federalism: Comparative Perspectives (2006), Volume 4
Dialogues on Foreign Relations in Federal Countries (2007), Volume 5
Dialogues on Local Government and Metropolitan Regions in Federal Countries (2007),
Volume 6

Select Global Dialogue publications are available in other languages including
Arabic, French, German, Portuguese and Spanish. For more information on
what is available, visit www.forumfed.org.

A Global Dialogue on Federalism
Booklet Series
Volume 7

DIALOGUES ON DIVERSITY AND UNITY IN FEDERAL COUNTRIES

EDITED BY RUPAK CHATTOPADHYAY AND ABIGAIL OSTIEN KAROS

Published by

 **Forum of Federations**

and

iacfs
INTERNATIONAL ASSOCIATION OF
CENTERS FOR FEDERAL STUDIES

© Forum of Federations, 2008
ISBN: 978-0-7735-3543-5

This publication was produced with generous financial support from the Government of Canada and the Swiss Agency for Development and Cooperation.

Library and Archives Canada Cataloguing in Publication

Dialogues on diversity and unity in federal countries / edited by Rupak Chattopadhyay and Abigail Ostien Karos.

(A global dialogue on federalism booklet series ; v. 7)
Includes bibliographical references.
ISBN 978-0-7735-3543-5

      1. Multiculturalism. 2. Federal government. 3. Nationalism. 4. Cultural pluralism. 5. Minorities. I. Chattopadhyay, Rupak II. Ostien, Abigail, 1971- III. International Association of Centers for Federal Studies IV. Forum of Federations V. Series: Global dialogue on federalism booklet series ; v. 7

JC312.D52 2009   321.02   C2008-906738-X

Printed and bound in Canada by Imprimerie Gauvin

Contents

Preface

We are pleased to introduce this booklet, Volume Seven in the Global Dialogue Booklet series, which is devoted to the topic of diversity and unity in twelve federal or federal-type countries. The featured countries are Australia, Belgium, Brazil, Canada, Ethiopia, Germany, India, Nigeria, Russia, Spain, Switzerland and the United States. Each of these countries has something unique to bring to the table of a topic that is often spoken of as "unity in diversity," pointing to a way beyond what is often assumed to be an inherent tension between the two. Diversity and unity – often the underlying reason behind countries adopting a federal structure in the first place – is behind many of the world's major news stories today. The theme's importance is also echoed in its selection as one of the four main topics considered in the Fourth International Conference on Federalism, held in New Delhi, India in 2007.

In due course the booklet will be followed by a more comprehensive book on the same topic, wherein the authors of the booklet explore the theme in further detail. Both publications, which are part of the Global Dialogue on Federalism Series, are the outcome of a greater project led by two partner organizations, the Forum of Federations and the International Association of Centers for Federal Studies. The program explores federal governance by theme and aims to bring experts together to inspire new ideas and fill a gap in the comparative literature on federal governance. After presenting the seventh booklet in less than three years, we recognize that these handy publications are becoming an indispensable reference document on their own, delivering instant comparative information on various topics in a concise format. It is therefore not surprising that the previous volumes proved to be very popular and have been translated in numerous languages, including most recently Arabic and Kurdish. As much as these booklets have their own standing, they also continue to fulfill their original task related to the books. The number of books sold is steadily growing and will increase this coming year with the publication of Volume 5,

"Foreign Relations in Federal Countries" and Volume 6, "Local Governments and Metropolitan Regions in Federal Countries."

The various aspects of the practice and the comparative perspectives of diversity and unity are described in country chapters entitled "Dialogue Insights." The chapters are introduced by a text of comparative reflections written by Luis Moreno and Cesar Colino. A glossary at the end of the booklet contributes to the accessible and educative nature of this publication. It is expected that Volume Seven will be translated into Arabic, French, German and Spanish, following in the footsteps of previous volumes.

The overarching theme in each of these articles is how to balance diversity with unity. Within that framework arise important questions such as: How does each country's unique history affect the way in which diversity is accommodated via the conduct of public policy, including ongoing claims for rectification of past wrongs? How does a country manage secessionist movements? Is multiculturalism viewed as part of a country's identity or something that threatens it? In other words, is it associated with a flowering of federalism, as in many countries in this booklet, or, as John Kincaid puts it in his article on the United States, a "devouring" of federalism? On what factors is "nationality" based and do citizens sometimes possess compound nationalities within one country? Are linguistic, religious, and racial differences manifested in territorial terms and if so, how does this affect the issue? What conditions help to set the stage for successful management of difference (i.e., affluence, a democratic culture, etc.)? Can any of these be imported to other countries? What policies have been put in place to either restrict (e.g., assimilation, racist immigration policies) or enhance diversity (e.g., accommodation, asymmetry)? What order of government is responsible for handling such diversity hotspots as education and immigration legislation? What is the relationship between federalism and democracy? This is an area which the Ethiopian, Swiss, Russian, Nigerian, and Brazilian articles discuss in particular. Ending on a note of hope, what is the basis for unity in the countries under discussion in this booklet?

The distinctiveness of the booklet and book series is based on the unique process by which the publications are generated. Each theme process entails multiple stages, starting with the selection of a "theme coordinator." It is this person's task to create an internationally comprehensive set of questions covering institutional provisions and how they work in practice, based on the most current research. These sets of questions are the foundation of the program, as they guide the dialogue at the roundtables and ensure consistency in the book chapters. The roundtables themselves are led by a "country coordinator," and are organized concurrently in twelve chosen countries. To create the most accurate picture of the situation in each country, the country coordinators invite a group of practicing and academic experts with diverse viewpoints and experience who are prepared to share with and learn from others in a non-politicized environment.

At the end of the day, the coordinators are equipped to write an article that reflects the highlights of the dialogue from each country roundtable. The articles presented here have been generated from such an exchange. Once each country has held its roundtable, representatives gather at an international roundtable to identify commonalities and differences and to generate new insights. Such insights are incorporated into the country chapters in the aforementioned theme book. The chapters reflect the fact that their authors were able to explore the theme from a global vantage point, resulting in a truly comparative exploration of the topic.

The success of the Global Dialogue Program depends fully on the engagement of a variety of organizations and dedicated individuals. For their generous financial support we would like to thank the Government of Canada and the Swiss Agency for Development and Cooperation. The International Roundtable in Brussels was made possible with generous support from the Committee of the Regions, of the European Union. We also wish in particular to acknowledge the experts who took part in the dialogue events for providing a diversity of perspectives that helped to shape the articles themselves. Luis Moreno and Cesar Colino, the Theme Coordinators, John Kincaid, Senior Editor of the book series, and the rest of the Global Dialogue Editorial Board have offered their invaluable advice and expertise. Thank you to Alan Fenna for doing the painstaking work of creating the glossary. We would like to acknowledge the support offered by several staff members at the Forum of Federations: Rhonda Dumas, Libby Johnston, Roderick Macdonell, Chris Randall, and Carl Stieren. We would like to thank the staff at Imprimerie Gauvin for their important assistance in the printing process. Finally, we thank the staff at McGill-Queen's University Press for offering their support and advice throughout the publication process.

The Global Dialogue on Federalism Series continues the Forum of Federations' tradition of publishing either independently or in partnership with other organizations. The Forum has produced a variety of books and multimedia material. For further information on the Forum's publications and activities, refer to the Forum's website at www.forumfed.org. The website contains links to other organizations and an on-line library which includes Global Dialogue articles and chapters. The increasing body of literature produced by the Forum of Federations and the International Association of Centers for Federal Studies aims to encourage practitioners and scholars to use the knowledge gained to inspire new solutions, thereby improving federal governance, and to join the many active participants around the world to expand and strengthen the growing international network on federalism. We welcome feedback and suggestions on how these series can be improved to serve this common goal.

Rupak Chattopadhyay and Abigail Karos, Editors
Forum of Federations

DIALOGUES ON DIVERSITY AND UNITY
IN FEDERAL COUNTRIES

Comparative Reflections on Diversity and Unity in Federal Countries

CÉSAR COLINO / LUIS MORENO

Old and new diversities around the world

Diversity seems to be one of the hottest issues in contemporary domestic and international politics. Debates about ethnic, national, linguistic, religious and economic diversity and its accommodation in viable and legitimate polities feature prominently in discussions among academics and practitioners of comparative politics, conflict resolution studies, political sociology and political theory. The recent emergence of transnational migrant networks brought about by globalization and the growing inequalities in the world economy, together with the claims by old minority groups and new social movements based on nationality, ethnicity, language or religion, pose increasing demands for old and new federal countries to achieve: (a) the full and equal inclusion and recognition of differences; (b) the protection and accommodation of minorities; and (c) the promotion of equal citizenship and participation in a common public sphere.

A long-standing diversity responsible for the formation of majorities and minorities and, therefore, a need for the accommodation in plural societies is language. As an identity marker, language is crucial not only in the building and self-definition of different communities, but also in the creation of a common sphere of public discourse. Religion is also crucial in the making and shaping of diverse groups and heterogeneous polities. Not surprisingly, the protection of linguistic and religious minorities has been an original terrain for the expansion of minority rights. Likewise, ethnicity or the existence of politically mobilized territorial or national self-defined identities in multiethnic or multinational societies represent a paramount challenge for the governance and accommodation of differences. Both national minorities and indigenous populations in settler societies have increasingly demanded self-government rights and the setting of separate institutions in their homeland territories where they often constitute the majority. They have also sought the establishment of reserved lands. In both cases, groups of this so-called deep diversity aspire to full jurisdiction over powers relevant to their cultural survival and nation-building projects. In many countries these diversities overlap with other non-territorial differences related to class, economic or gender, which can be more or less politicized.

Furthermore, the emergence of new diversities as a result of individual or group migrations can also be witnessed around the world. Consequently, new minorities seek greater recognition of their cultural differences and their inclusion in common institutions. In federal countries, immigration affects the cultural integrity of their various constituent units. These may feel threatened by new minorities, which may cause tensions between the demands of minority nations and the cultural rights of ethnic migrants.

Diversity in federal countries: multiple configurations of old and new diversities

As the 12 cases analyzed in this booklet show, not all federal countries reflect the same degree and types of diversity. Although not all traditional federations were originally designed to accommodate all these kinds of diversities or to empower ethnic or linguistic minorities, federal arrangements seem increasingly the preferred and most able means to conciliate respect for diversity with a common purpose or unity. Particular federal arrangements and policies based on particular configurations of social and political diversities deal differently with the accommodation of differences, the management of conflicts, and the establishment of a legitimate and stable order.

Historical and socio-political dimensions

Several factors such as history, geography, demography and economy have determined the evolution of the 12 cases presented in this booklet. There are several dimensions that constitute the social basis of federal countries and the main distinguishing features of each of them:

i.   The extent to which there is one predominant cultural / ethnic group or a variety of territorial minorities. In some cases, political identities are strong and socially mobilized (Switzerland) or are easily assimilated into the majoritarian cultural group (Germany or USA). In some cases federations face mobilized aboriginal people or indigenous populations ('First Nations' in Australia or Canada).

ii. The extent to which diversities appear associated with territory and ethnic, linguistic or religious minorities or majorities within the federation's constituent units. In some instances, ethnolinguistic or cultural groups are concentrated within a particular geographic area and minorities are attached to identifiable territories of their own (Russia,

Canada or Switzerland). In others, groups are dispersed throughout the territory of the federation (Brazil or the USA), or diversities may cut across different territories and groups (India or Nigeria).

iii. The number of constituent units forming the federal country. Some federations have developed by increasing the number of units and some have remained with two or three units reflecting mainly bicommunal cleavages (US or Switzerland vs. Belgium).

iv. The extent to which there are significant regional or non-state-wide parties ruling in component units or represented at the federal parliament (Spain), and the extent to which those parties may form coalitions at the federal level and command enough legitimacy or fail to represent the whole population in the various units (Belgium).

v. The extent to which socio-economic resources and group interests are territorially concentrated – or controlled by specific groups – and economic development diverges sharply among the different constituent units (Brazil, Australia, Ethiopia or Nigeria).

vi. The extent to which different kinds of diversity in the federal countries reinforce – or cut across – each other. In Switzerland, for example, religious, language or communal identities do not necessarily overlap. In Ethiopia differences are compounded, which may make accommodation harder.

vii. The extent to which there are secessionist movements in the federal country and the extent to which they resort to violence or terrorism to achieve their demands (Russia or Spain).

viii. The extent to which different ethnocultural or territorial groups or individuals are over / under-represented in the institutions of the federation's public administration, military, judiciary, business or intelligentsia (Russia, Nigeria).

Diversity in diversity

The configuration of diversity is also diverse in itself. A review of the 12 cases included in this booklet show the shortcomings of the usual differentiations between homogeneous and heterogeneous, national and plural, mononational and multinational federations, as well as the distinction between ethnic and territorial federalism. The picture is one of diversity in diversity, which defies easy categorization. This notwithstanding, it seems useful to group several configurations of diversities in separate categories that may indicate an increasing degree of challenge for institutional design, stability and legitimacy. Ranging from less to more politicized old and new diversity, we may identify six distinct groups:

1. National federations with historical and newly created political units, mainly monolingual with new groups of immigrants unequally distributed across units. Political parties are predominantly nation-wide (Germany).

2. National federations with indigenous populations, old immigrant groups, different religions, a dominant *lingua franca* and predominant nation-wide parties, and where new diversities are not territorially concentrated (USA, Australia, Brazil).
3. Multilingual, multi-unit recent federal countries, with a dominant *lingua franca* and national identity but with several mobilized minority national groups and increasing new religious and cultural diversity. Strong nation-wide parties but also strong sub-national parties ruling some constituent units (Spain).
4. Multilingual and multicultural federations (largely bi- or tri-communal) with no national *lingua franca,* with strong local identities compatible with a nation-wide identity. There are weak – or non-existent – nation-wide parties and there is increasing new polyethnic diversity within the constituent units (Belgium, Switzerland).
5. Bilingual federations where several national groups, including indigenous populations, and with one of them dominant, are mobilized. Non state-wide parties are strong and there is an increasing polyethnicity due to new immigration (Canada).
6. Multiethnic, multilingual and multireligious federal countries with multiple constituent units which are designed mainly along ethnic or linguistic lines, although there may be one *lingua franca.* There are different configurations of party systems, strong socioeconomic disparities and large internal migration flows (Russia, India, Nigeria, Ethiopia).

The federal governance of diversity: design options and institutional responses
Basic federal institutional arrangements for self-government and shared government
In response to the various configurations of diversity and in order to preserve unity and manage diversity, different institutional responses and strategies can be observed in the federal countries under analysis. The two basic functions that federal institutions aim to achieve; self government, autonomy and accommodation, on one side, and shared rule, integration and participation, on the other, vary in our 12 cases:

Self-government and autonomy arrangements
Among the various self-government arrangements for the management of diversity in the analyzed federal countries, the following can be identified: (a) a separation and exclusivity of powers and own-sources of revenue for the constituent units (Switzerland), (b) a decentralization of powers for cultural or nation-building policies (Belgium, Spain, Canada), and (c) an integration of the constituent units in constitutional amendment procedures (Switzerland, Canada). Asymmetries, the constitutionally entrenched special treatment or powers of some units, are also used to accommodate diversities (e.g. the special fiscal and tax arrangements for the Basque Country in Spain).

Integration and participation at the federal (central) institutions
In some federal countries second chambers directly represent consti-tuent
units at the federal level. In others they are designed to give voice
to certain minorities. Also formal and informal – *de jure* or *de facto* –
conso-ciational arrangements are often put in place: (a) arrangements to
guarantee various groups a place in national decision-making (Belgium),
(b) the representation of all groups or territories in the federal cabinet
(Canada, Switzerland, Belgium), (c) collective or rotating presidencies
(Switzerland); (d) the conventional allocation of specific portfolios to
politicians coming from certain units (Spain), or (e) electoral systems
devised to produce a sufficient degree of proportionality to reflect existing
minorities (Belgium, Switzerland, Spain).

Specific responses to multiple diversities and to the achievement of unity
Institutional responses to tackle specific types of diversity are also articulated in federal countries showing an array of strategies and values in their
treatment of diversity. Two main approaches can be distinguished. When
managing diversity some federal countries tend to emphasize integration
and inclusion of ethno-cultural differences and its privatization by means
of securing individual rights, while others seek to publicly recognize those
differences and empower the groups with collective rights. The former
promote citizens' equality before the law and generally oppose the institutional recognition of group identities, although accepting and respecting
cultural or other diversity in private realms (US, Germany, Spain). The
latter advocates the representation of groups and minorities as such, with
full institutional recognition of differences (Ethiopia, Nigeria, Switzerland).
Some federations use these two approaches in combination (India,
Canada, Australia).

Ethnic/national diversity
Some federal countries disregard ethnic cleavages and, as a result, territorial boundaries of the constituent units cut across ethnic groups (USA,
Brazil). Others make visible the territorial distribution of ethnic groups
(Belgium, India or Ethiopia). In some other cases the boundaries of the
constituent units reflect the territorial ethno-linguistic diversity, although
the largest ethnocultural group is also distributed across many of those
units (Canada, Nigeria, Russia, Switzerland). Some federal constitutions
recognize the possibility and flexibility for re-designing the internal
boundaries along ethnic or ethnolinguistic lines, or adding additional
units to the federation which, sometimes, are carved out of existing units
(India, Switzerland). Giving different constitutional status to the various types
of constituent units is also an option for managing diversity (Russia).
A further option can be labeled as one of 'constitutional ambiguity'. Leaving
the constitutional definition of the federal arrangements ambiguous may

allow several groups to interpret their membership differently. This may avoid the 'swallowing' of a particular definition of diversity favored by majoritarian groups (Canada, Spain).

In federal countries where a minority group is a majority in a territorial unit, some citizens belonging to the federation's larger group may face a minority situation. In such a situation, constitutions can provide for a protection of the 'minorities within the minorities' (Canada). Likewise, and in order to 'pre-empt' forced territorial assimilation of the constituent units, the right of secession can be constitutionally recognized (Ethiopia).

Linguistic/religious diversity

Most federal countries aim at achieving unity in their shared political institutions by the establishment of one official language, or the promotion of a common *lingua franca*. In multi-lingual countries, beyond the constitutional recognition of the local languages, and the right for citizens to use their own vernacular languages, a common *lingua franca* is used widespread so that different peoples can easily communicate (Amharic in Ethiopia, Castilian-Spanish in Spain, English in India and Nigeria, Russian in the Russian Federation).

Other specific arrangements to deal with linguistic or ethnic diversity are of a non-territorial nature. They deal at an individual level disregarding citizens' place of residence (e.g. communities in Belgium or 'national-cultural autonomy" for some groups in Russia).

Concerning religion there is also a considerable variety of diversity, ranging from the secularist exclusion of all religious matters from the public sphere to corporatist forms of religious inclusion in the federal or constituent units' institutions. In some cases, some constituent units may recognize religious law (such as Sharia in Nigeria).

Migration and new diversity

New diversity brought about by individual migrants is generally dealt with through the traditional mechanisms of minority rights – which may be constitutionally protected – and by citizenship regulations. In some cases different orders of government may grant citizenship status to immigrants (Switzerland). In recent times, an increasing number of federal countries have implemented policies of 'multiculturalism' so that individual inclusion and recognition of cultural differences can be simultaneously achieved. Such policies go beyond mere non-discrimination and seek: (a) to extend anti-racism policies; (b) to reform educational curricula to incorporate the inputs and contributions of immigrant groups; (c) to fund publicly the cultural practices of immigrant groups.

In many federal countries, some constituent units have been active in using their self-government powers to secure the incorporation and integration of immigrants by means of implementing their own education, labor and language policies (Canada, Belgium, Spain). Along these lines, sub-national governments have often been keen in requiring migrants to learn the vernacular language of the constituent unit (e.g. Québec in Canada). In other federations, language and citizenship tests have been established for immigrants (Germany).

Concluding remarks

In sum, federal countries face a number of dilemmas when confronting old and new types of diversity. Other than the long-standing tensions between autonomy and cooperation, flexibility and stability, centrifugal and centripetal trends, federations have to reconcile one major challenge which is common to all cases concerned: the recognition of differences and the means to respect them while articulating unity, trust and solidarity among citizens and groups. Such a course of action implies that democratic federal polities ought to provide a common public space leaving room for diverse cultural practices and identities to exist and develop. Federal countries also seek to guarantee the conciliation of the rights of the individuals – no matter where they live – and the recognition of minorities as groups. Most federal countries have proved that diversity is not a threat for their survival and prosperity, and that the recognition, accommodation and integration of ethnic, linguistic or religious minorities are compatible with legitimacy, national unity and social cohesion.

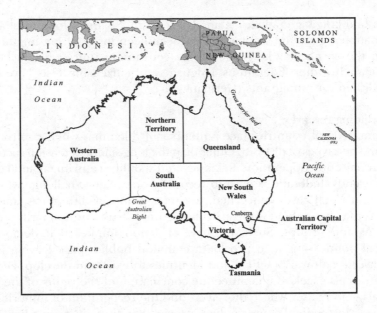

Unity and Diversity in Federal Australia

NICHOLAS ARONEY

Australia is one of the oldest federations in the world. Formed in 1901 when the six British colonies of the Australian continent agreed to unite in a federal commonwealth under the Crown of Great Britain, the federation was largely modelled upon three earlier federal states: the American, the Canadian, and the Swiss. Like the United States and Canada, Australia is a nation of immigrants. Over the course of the nineteenth and twentieth centuries, successive waves of first British, then European, and more recently Asian migrants, have made the country one of the most ethnically diverse in the world. However, unlike many federations – such as the Canadian and the Swiss – Australia's ethno-cultural diversity is not, for the most part, territorially-defined. Regional differences in terms of socio-economic conditions are, by comparison, much more pronounced. Each of the six Australian states presents a roughly similar ethno-cultural diversity, whether this diversity is defined in terms of reported ancestry, religion, or language, whereas there are significant differences in the socio-economic conditions of the various states.

When the six Australian colonies federated in 1901, they did so in order to give effect to political diversity, rather than ethno-cultural diversity. The leading idea at the time was that federalism would enable the people of each state to continue to govern themselves in most matters, while having a share in a national government through which they could govern the affairs of the continent as a whole. In 1901 the Australian states were populated by people almost entirely of British origin and the diversity that existed lay in the very real differences between persons of English, Scottish, and Irish ancestry, together with a not insignificant number of Chinese and South Pacific labourers, and what was already by then a relatively small proportion of indigenous peoples. As far as most of the voting population was concerned, it was believed that Australia should remain a country populated by people of mostly British origin. One of the very first policies to be implemented by the Australian Commonwealth government after forming the federation was to institute what became known as the "White Australia Policy," a policy intended to minimize non-white immigration in order to preserve Anglo Celtic culture and reduce competition for working-class jobs.

The White Australia Policy remained in place for the first half of the 20th century, but after the Second World War, Australia increasingly opened itself up to non-British immigrants, mostly from western and southern European countries such as Germany, Italy, and Greece. During the 1950s the government implemented an official policy of assimilation, under which migrants of non-British origin were expected to adopt the English language and the dominant culture. This policy also extended, in theory, to Australia's indigenous peoples, as previous tendencies to exclude and separate Australian Aborigines from the mainstream gave way to attempts to assimilate them through education and "protection," including the removal of many indigenous children from their parents. During the 1950s and 1960s, as various elements of the White Australia Policy were officially abandoned, Australian government policies in relation to both immigration and Aborigines became, formally at least, racially and culturally neutral. Pursuant to a 1967 referendum, the power to make laws with respect to Aborigines was transferred to the Commonwealth. The referendum result was widely seen as an acknowledgement that indigenous peoples were entitled to the same rights as all Australians.

Although Britain remains the major source of Australian immigration, increasing numbers of migrants from a wider range of countries in Europe and Asia form the context in which from the 1970s onwards opinion leaders advocated the adoption of multicultural policies to encourage immigrants to maintain and preserve their distinct ethno-cultural identities. Official multiculturalism coincided with the recognition of aboriginal land rights and the establishment and development in the 1980s and 1990s of institutions intended to accommodate indigenous peoples' aspirations for self-government. Yet throughout this period the basic living standards and economic opportunities of most indigenous Australians remained substantially lower than most other Australians. In response to allegations of corruption and misuse of power, the federal government has dismantled many indigenous self-governing institutions over the past decade and intervened recently in Aboriginal communities in the Northern Territory in order to address reported problems of endemic abuse and deprivation. Moreover, even though by international standards there is a high level of cultural integration in Australia, in the last decade Australians have engaged in a renewed debate over multicultural policy and Australia's capacity to absorb comparatively large numbers of migrants from a wide variety of ethno-cultural backgrounds. Maintaining an appropriate balance between ethno-cultural diversity and national unity remains a highly disputed question in Australian politics.

Today, there are only two major exceptions to the important general observation that diversity in Australia is non-territorial in character. The first exception can be observed in the fact that a quarter of Australia's indigenous peoples live in highly remote communities located in the vast inner reaches of the Northern Territory, New South Wales, Queensland, Western Australia, and South Australia, while another 20 percent reside in outer regional areas. In this context, and given the very substantial problems faced by indigenous peoples when measured in terms of basic living standards, physical health and economic opportunity, one of the more important diversity issues faced by Australian governments concerns the future of aboriginal autonomy and self-determination.

The second respect in which Australia's diversity has a territorial dimension concerns the significantly different economic capacities and prospects of the various states, regions, and localities of the country. In certain respects, these differences are related to the ethno-cultural characteristics of the regions or localities in question, but for the most part these areas are themselves ethno-culturally diverse. The federal government has taken over the main sources of taxation revenue and distributed money to the states, partly to equalize the financial capacities of the states and partly to advance federal government policies at the expense of the states. Equalization policies frequently give rise to complaints from the wealthier states – especially New South Wales – and the fastest growing states such as Queensland and Western Australia, that they are unfairly subsidizing poorer states like Tasmania and South Australia. There are also long-standing concerns about the lack of symmetry in the balance of power between the Commonwealth and the states. Indeed, fiscal imbalance, asymmetries of power, a lack of policy diversity, and unequal economic development represent what might be regarded as the most pressing issues confronting the capacity of the Australian federation to deliver genuine policy diversity in the context of a national economy operating in an increasingly global environment.

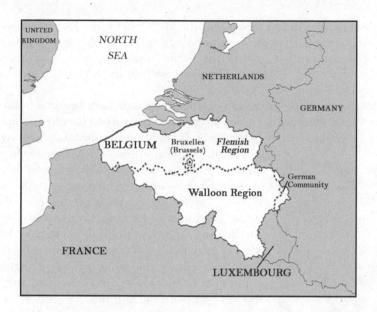

Belgium: Unity Challenged by Diversity

FRANK DELMARTINO / HUGUES DUMONT /
SÉBASTIEN VAN DROOGHENBROECK

Belgium is a newcomer on the scene of federal countries. Only in 1993 did the Constitution acknowledge the federal character of the institutional reforms that have fundamentally restructured the former unitary state. Structural reform, however, has been taking place since 1970 – a process that has not yet reached its final stage. Presently, Belgium is confronting a major political crisis that questions its identity as a federal country. The possibility of confederalism – a voluntary union – or, ultimately, secession, looms large in the public debate. Although the future of the country is unpredictable, Belgium remains an interesting case for comparative research, since it has adopted a wide variety of institutional innovations explicitly designed to accommodate diversity.

An ongoing process

From the very first years of the kingdom of Belgium, the dominant class that had instigated the revolution of 1830 was involved in developing a sense of national consciousness. However, this shaping of a Belgian identity centred on francophone culture to the neglect of the culture and language of the majority Flemish-speaking population. In the mid-19th century, Flemish cultural organizations began to contest the general disregard of their cultural heritage. And by the turn of the 20th century, the Flemish movement had articulated its struggle for the recognition of a Flemish linguistic and cultural identity with a goal of the social and economic emancipation of Flanders. Since the 1930s, the Flemish have put forth claims for more and more political autonomy.

Although in recent years most of these demands have been met, the quest for autonomy has become more diverse and has spread to other component parts of Belgian society since the 1960s. In addition to cultural autonomy, social and economic development policies have been put on the agenda. In reaction to these broad demands, the state has responded by creating two types of overlapping federated entities: Communities, divided by the languages of Flemish, French, and German, and Regions, known as the Walloon Region, Flemish Region and Brussels-Capital Region. The former deals with education, language usage regulation, cultural and "person-related" matters; the latter focuses on economic and territory-related issues.

> This never-ending story of reform after reform is inevitably shattering the *Pax Belgica*. It signals that no consensus has yet been reached on a constitutional model that accommodates the centrifugal tendencies in Flanders with the status-quo advocated by Brussels and Wallonia.

In spite of these accommodations, there are still demands – especially from the Flemish – for a more encompassing autonomy, thereby challenging the relevance of the federal order. This never-ending story of reform after reform is inevitably shattering the *Pax Belgica*. It signals that no consensus has yet been reached on a constitutional model that accommodates the centrifugal tendencies in Flanders with the status-quo advocated by Brussels and Wallonia.

Asymmetry

Over the years Communities and Regions have developed into fairly well-functioning sub-national authorities, with their own governments. The main problem challenging the survival of this complex system is the emergence of a sense of nationhood in Flanders. Not coincidentally, the institutions of the Flemish-speaking Community and the Flemish Region have merged into a single framework, simply called Flanders, whereas the French-speaking Community and the Walloon Region are still separated from an institutional point of view. Moreover, by insisting on the interrelated character of different policy areas, Flanders is claiming an all-round competency for dealing with the manifold dimensions of governance. Therefore, the asymmetry between Flanders and the other Regions is not only of an institutional character; in its self-perception, Flanders is a full-fledged authority with the political profile of a nation-state. Recently, the Walloon and Brussels Regions have coordinated their policies and shared their political leadership. This alliance, called *Wallonie-Bruxelles,* is signalling the de facto bipolarity of the country.

Bipolarity
Belgium is perceived by the outside world and by most of its citizens as a bipolar country composed of Flemish speakers and *francophones*. The German-speaking community, while highly respected and a full-fledged partner constitutionally, is not considered a relevant actor on the national political scene. However, this bipolar nation is not only divided by the use of different languages. The cultural-linguistic cleavage is an epiphenomenon, hiding a deeper divide. What is the national character of Belgium? The northern and southern regions of the country would answer that question differently, pointing to their different political discourses and distinct styles of policy-making. It is significant that the former national political parties, including the ones with a clear ideological profile, all split up in the 1970s and 80s. The non-existence of national political parties results in a vulnerability for the federal system. No politician, not even the federal prime minister, is democratically legitimized in the country as a whole. This leaves the Belgian legacy politically unprotected. As a solution, many sides advocate the introduction of a federal constituency where political leaders can address the nation in its entirety.

Brussels
A Region of its own, the capital city of Belgium both unites and divides the country. Fittingly it is situated in the middle of the country serving as both a cross-road and dividing line between Flanders and Wallonia. However, if secession between the North and the South came to pass, it is quite clear that the *francophone* majority in Brussels would prefer to stay united with Wallonia. For its part Flanders is linked to the capital not only historically, but also economically and socially; relinquishing Brussels is not an option. The mere existence of Brussels is the best guarantee for the Belgian "marriage of convenience" to persevere. In spite of this, the complex institutional setting guaranteeing the Flemish representation in the Brussels Region, and the permanence of the current boundaries of the capital Region despite the marked presence of *francophones* in its periphery, are among the strongest disintegrating forces in the North-South dialogue.

Exclusive competencies and co-operative federalism
In Belgian federalism, the principle of jurisdictional exclusivity, or only one authority having jurisdiction for any given matter, is central. This policy has not prevented dialogue and cooperation between the different governmental actors. On the contrary, diverse forms of organic cooperation (i.e., joint bodies), procedural cooperation, and conventional cooperation (i.e., intergovernmental agreements), have been increasing significantly over the last 20 years. However, despite these forms of cooperative federalism, there is a demand on the Flemish side for a more encompassing autonomy. Given its policy of jurisdictional exclusivity, the Belgian system of division of powers may shift from a federal into a confederal model.

Brazil:
Diversity and Unity beyond Territories

MARCUS FARO DE CASTRO /
GILBERTO MARCOS ANTONIO RODRIGUES

Although there are no secession claims by internal groups, and in spite of the fact that it has a single national official and *de facto* language, the Brazilian federation still faces regional socioeconomic inequalities and has continually failed to effectively promote broad implementation of minority rights.

The 1988 Constitution was adopted after two decades of military dictatorship. The 20 years of authoritarian rule were characterized by the deployment of economic policies that propelled economic growth but did not address concerns about equality. Economic development during these years benefited the few and not the many. Moreover the decision makers of the so-called "Brazilian Economic Miracle" during the 1970s and 1980s acted on the premise that minorities, and above all indigenous peoples, should be assimilated on the pretext of "unity." One of the main intentions of the drafters of the 1988 Constitution was that it should stand as a new symbol of the prevalence of inalienable rights and as an instrument that would recast Brazilian institutions in a fresh new democratic mould, thus leaving behind all institutional structures of the authoritarian past.

As part of the effort of such institution-building, the 1988 Constitution adopted a "three-tiered model" of federation, under which the central government, states, and municipalities were each granted the constitutional status of federal entities endowed with roughly symmetric powers. This innovative reform of the federal system included devolution of powers to the states, and especially to municipalities, in conjunction with redistribution schemes under fiscal federalism. In addition, the new emphasis on federal decentralization offered, together with other conditions, specific incentives for the addition of new municipalities, which in now number 5,562.

Yet, despite the new stress on federal decentralization, mainly by means of imparting federal status to municipalities, the new three-tiered federation has continued to suffer from difficulties inherited from the country's political past. The ongoing nature of such difficulties has to do with how national unity relates to sub-national diversity (and potentially to empowerment) through the federal institutional system. In its concrete practice and implications, the federal system becomes a means to keep significant minorities hostage to socioeconomic marginalization and political disempowerment. These minorities include Afro-Brazilians, indigenous peoples, *quilombolas* (communities of descendants of black slaves who escaped their plantations before slavery was abolished in 1888), and Roma, better known as gypsies.

> In its concrete practice and implications, the federal system becomes a means to keep significant minorities hostage to socioeconomic marginalization and political disempowerment.

One key issue to understanding the limitations of the Brazilian federation in promoting diversity rights is that devolution of powers has characteristically been territorial – states and municipalities were empowered but groups were not. Diversity rights refer to claims through which the assertion of one's social and economic rights and expression of one's identity are combined to promote self-worth. It is striking, though not unheard of, that territorially circumscribed local authority in Brazil has given rise to multiple forms of oppression that pre-empt the full enjoyment of diversity rights.

But why is it that the reform of the federal system, implying greater devolution to municipalities, did not bring about a deeper transformation of policy making in Brazil? The answers seem to point to the inability of local authorities in many regions, including the police, judicial courts, and prosecutors, to prevent widespread violation of basic human rights, such as torture in prisons and violent suppression of dissent in rural areas. Local authorities have also failed to come up with the appropriate institutional means of governing and carrying out programs in ways other than simple territorial devolution. In many instances territorially-based devolution has only aided the spread of basic human rights violations. This has brought about an urgent need for the central government to establish a federal witness protection program in an attempt to curb the power of oppressive local elites.

Although the 1988 Constitution has formally recognized diversity rights in its structures of governance, it has failed to incorporate trans-territorial institutional arrangements that would foster substantive recognition and implementation of such rights. The 1988 Constitution sets out the existence of concurrent powers, which are shared by the central government, the states, and the municipalities; however, it does not adequately address the need to promote multi-level, trans-sectoral coordination of policies. One striking example can be found in the inadequate federal policies coordinated by the central government that are provided to indigenous populations. In practice such policies do not address the cultural and identity needs of such peoples. As a consequence, important content is lacking in policies that target indigenous communities, such as dietary requirements in right-to-food policies, bilingual education, culturally-sensitive health care approaches, and so on.

Brazil needs to effectively promote diversity rights without posing a threat to national unity. It could do so by implementing international treaties and human rights codes that Brazil had signed, especially if it implemented them in a way that was non-territorial or trans-territorial. Such a move would replace territorial devolution with alternative, trans-territorial arrangements. In this sense it is remarkable that, having signed many international treaties that could have generated internationally and federally articulated policies, Brazil did not take advantage of such opportunities – and in some cases actual legal mandates – to develop international, diversity rights enhancing programs in areas related to international legislation. These include: normative instruments of Mercosur (South American common market); Convention no. 169 of the International Labor Organization (Convention Concerning Indigenous and Tribal Peoples in Independent Countries); and Convention on Biological Diversity (traditional dependence on biological resources and protection of traditional knowledge).

Finally, one important innovation must be singled out that provides new possibilities of developing multilevel, trans-territorial federal cooperation. This is the creation of the so-called "public consortia," introduced in 2005. Such public consortia seem to be a promising instrument of diversity-enhancing governance, since they create legal entities that congregate multilevel government representatives in more *ad hoc,* asymmetrical, and flexible efforts of trans-territorial cooperation for policy making, such as in the field of infrastructure services in metropolitan areas. The results of this form of cooperation may prove to be an important step forward in the promotion of diversity rights.

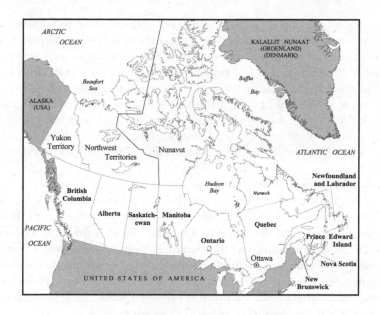

Unity and Diversity in Canada:
A Preliminary Assessment

ALAIN-G. GAGNON / RICHARD SIMEON

Balancing unity and diversity has preoccupied Canadians throughout their history and continues to do so today. Yet by international standards, Canada is considered a success. As one of the world's oldest and most stable federations, Canada has managed to deal with several dimensions of diversity simultaneously. It is a multinational country, responding to the province of Quebec's sense of nationhood and to Aboriginal people's conception of themselves as First Nations. It is a highly regional country – a "federal society" – with important provincial identities, and with large regional differences in terms of demography, population, economy and wealth. It is a country of immigrants, increasingly characterized by a diverse, multicultural population.

Several elements of the Canadian model stand out. First, Canadians have debated their differences – even the possibility that one member state, Quebec, might secede from the country – in ways that are peaceful, civil, and respectful of democratic values. Second, in responding to diversity, Canada has been what we might call an ongoing "negotiated" country, rather than a country of revolution or single majority domination. Third, both Canadian law and historical political practice have been based on the premise that unity is best achieved through the recognition and accommodation of difference. The fundamental values underpinning the Canadian model were well-stated by the Supreme Court of Canada in a landmark 1998 decision. The Court held that democracy, federalism, constitutionalism and the rule of law and respect for minority rights were, and must remain, the guiding principles of the Canadian federation. Many worry however that too much emphasis on diversity and not enough on shared Canadian values raises the question of social cohesion and solidarity; where is the "glue" that binds individuals and communities together?

Canada and Quebec, French and English
The only cleavage that could end the Canadian experiment is a rift between English and French-speaking Canadians, expressed as the division between Quebec and the "Rest of Canada." French-speaking Canadians make up about one quarter of the Canadian population. About 80 percent of those French-speaking Canadians live in Quebec where they constitute more than 85 percent of the population. Thus, while there are important linguistic minorities both within and outside Quebec, the linguistic division is primarily expressed in territorial terms.

Aboriginal Canadians
Canada, like the United States and Australia, was a classic settler society in which Europeans pushed the indigenous peoples to the margins. The legacies of this history remain today. Aboriginal peoples – Indians, Métis, and Inuit – make up only about three percent of the population but make a strong claim for long-delayed justice. This is based on the historic wrongs of their dispossession, and on historic social outcomes characterized by high rates of unemployment, poverty, disease, and social distress.

In the modern period, Aboriginal political mobilization began in the 1960s in reaction against proposed new Canadian policy to assimilate them fully into mainstream life. Aboriginal peoples reacted to maintain their societies and cultures, to regain control over land and resources, and to acquire a measure of self government. They defined themselves as First Nations, with an inherent right to self-government and with a desire to interact with other Canadians on a nation-to-nation basis. A Canadian Royal Commission strongly endorsed these views in the mid 1990s. A series of decisions by Canadian courts have supported Aboriginal claims and enhanced their bargaining power. The revisions to the Canadian Constitution of 1982 recognized Aboriginal status and provided for constitutional protection of past and future treaties. However, these changes have little effect on the majority of Aboriginal peoples, who now live in urban areas. Many Canadians view relations with Aboriginal peoples as the darkest stain on Canada's historical record of accommodation of diversity.

Region

Federalism, conferring considerable policy and fiscal autonomy to the provinces, is the primary institutional mechanism for managing regional differences. Intergovernmental relations conducted through the mechanisms of executive federalism have generally been a successful means of negotiating the accommodation of differences. But this process has become competitive and adversarial in recent years, with each order of government focused on protecting its own turf and bickering over financial arrangements. The underlying concern is that the Canadian form of federalism exacerbates rather than ameliorates matters at the regional level.

Multiculturalism

From its beginning, Canada has been a country of immigrants. For most of its history, Canadian policy favored immigration from Europe and was explicitly racist. In the 1970s, Canada, like other countries, removed most of the discriminatory elements from its policies and significantly increased the number of immigrants it welcomed. Today, Canada has one of the most open immigration policies in the world to the degree that it has embraced multiculturalism as a fundamental and defining characteristic of the country. This is reflected in the Constitution Act, 1982, which includes a clause requiring that the Charter of Rights and Freedoms be interpreted in light of the multicultural character of Canada, and in the Multiculturalism Act of 1988 that defines multiculturalism as fundamental to Canadian identity. With respect to social integration, these policies have been very successful.

There is some evidence that the celebrated Canadian commitment to multiculturalism may be fraying at least at the edges in recent debates, but there is little evidence of a fundamental shift away from a commitment to multiculturalism.

These are major successes, but complacency is to be avoided. Some immigrant groups have done much better professionally and economically than others. Cities that have received the majority of immigrants continue to have difficulties in integrating new Canadians, and providing services in multiple languages. Cities need to play a larger role in immigration policy and need more support to enact their role in integration. Canadians are debating how to reflect the universal values and individual rights embodied in the Charter of Rights and Freedoms with the collective rights of Aboriginal peoples and Quebecers. There is some evidence that the celebrated Canadian commitment to multiculturalism may be fraying at least at the edges in recent debates, but there is little evidence of a fundamental shift away from a commitment to multiculturalism, or, as Quebec calls it, *interculturalism*.

Conclusion and Lessons

Canada's is a good news story, despite its flaws. Multiple diversities can be accommodated and managed peacefully and democratically. Canadians' ability to manage their differences has depended on a number of benign conditions that do not necessarily prevail elsewhere, especially in developing countries, namely: a democratic culture; respect for the rule of law; a tradition of negotiation and compromise, affluence and a prosperous economy; extensive social infrastructure and high levels of education and peaceful relations with the neighboring U.S. Nevertheless, there are other elements in the Canadian experience that others might consider. These include the provisions of Canadian multiculturalism and Quebec's *interculturalism;* Canada's tradition as a welfare state; its ability to embrace asymmetrical federalism; and to have elaborated, with the help of the Supreme Court, clear principles that would prevail in the event of either a coming together or a dissolution of the country.

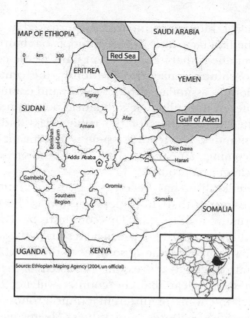

MAP OF ETHIOPIA — SAUDI ARABIA — Red Sea — ERITREA — YEMEN — Tigray — SUDAN — Afar — Gulf of Aden — Benishan gul-Gum — Amara — Dire Dawa — Addis Ababa — Harari — Gambela — Oromia — Southern Region — Somalia — SOMALIA — UGANDA — KENYA — Source: Ethiopian Maping Agency (2004, un official)

Federalism and the Management
of Diversity in Ethiopia

MOHAMMED HABIB / ASSEFA FISEHA

Ethiopia is widely known for having successfully escaped western colonial domination. Over the last three decades, this ancient African state has gone through a wave of revolutionary changes leading to the demise of both the imperial era and the military regime of 1974 to 1991. Following the collapse of the centralized unitary era in May 1991, the country was restructured as federal, constituted by nine regional states and two autonomous cities, with a significant degree of commitment to accommodate ethno-linguistic diversity and related sub-national interests. The transition from a centralized unitary state to the current federal arrangement was brought about by liberation movements represented by ethno-linguistic groups in different parts of the country who forcefully dismantled and then rebuilt the nation's structure. These liberation movements dominated the process of restructuring the state into a federation.

  But the "national question" has remained one of the major political challenges in Ethiopia for more than half a century. The excessive concentration of power and resources at the centre and the insistence upon ethnic homogenization resulted in a series of historical grievances on the part of the different ethno-linguistic groups and cultural communities.

For a long period Ethiopia was incorrectly portrayed as a mono-cultural society and unified unitary state. In fact, Ethiopia has more than 80 ethno-linguistic communities inhabiting different parts of the country. None of these groups constitutes a majority. Previously, the central government used its institutions to assimilate diverse groups and communities into the culture and values of the ruling class. Political power and resources were largely distributed to members of the ruling class and specific ethnic groups or communities. The federal system is now meant to address these historical shortcomings and respond to the aspirations of the country's different ethno-linguistic groups.

Fortunately, federalism has become a point of national consensus; virtually all sides agree that the federal option is the only viable and reasonable alternative for Ethiopia. This consensus has come as a result of the change in attitudes toward the practical results of the system. In the initial stages, there was anxiety among some as to the possible consequences of the reforms introduced to address the grievances of the different ethnic groups. Now, it seems clear that the country will not fracture because of the increased freedoms of different ethnic groups to express their sub-national identities, cultures, and values. Meanwhile, differences of perspectives still exist on several issues such as the protection of minorities at both the regional and federal orders and the devolution of power and resources to the states.

A major concern relates to the interests and prospects of minorities in each of the nine federated regional states of the federation and is likely to remain a source of tension for some time. Given the inexperience of the state functionaries at the local order and the absence of effective democratic institutions and civil society in the country, certain measures are incumbent on the federal authorities to ensure uniform implementation of the rights enshrined in the constitution. On the other hand, the legitimate interests of the different ethnic groups to administer their localities need be respected as long as democratic rules and principles prevail. The challenge is in striking a reasonable balance between these competing interests.

Another topic of debate relates to the mechanism for protecting the interests of the different ethnic groups and communities at the federal order. Ethiopian federalism seeks to accommodate the interests of the different ethnic groups at the centre. Contrary to common practice, the second federal house, otherwise known as the House of Federation, does not take part in the legislative process. Thus, the smaller minorities are left at a disadvantage. The absence of pluralistic political participation in the House amounts to denying it of a vital resource to promote the interests of the peoples of the country. Consequently, some call for direct election of the members of the House as opposed to the current practice of state organs choosing the House delegates.

The issue of decentralization of power and resources to the regional states has attracted considerable attention. The federal Constitution grants considerable autonomy to the regions. Perhaps the most controversial is the right granted to the nationalities to secede. However, since Ethiopia is currently under the rule of one dominant party, there is some scepticism as to the freedom of state government actors in safeguarding the autonomy and interests of their constituencies within the frame of the Constitution. Some argue that despite the constitutional autonomy of the regional states, the political reality simply continues the traditional control by the centre. The existing financial situation of the states also shows an over-dependency on federal subsidies – due less to the Constitution itself and more to party structures. It has been argued that the prevalent political culture has not been in favour of power sharing and participation. This means that a key challenge is for the federal system to inculcate and promote the growth of participatory and democratic political culture in the country. Currently, there is clear and broad interest in protecting the autonomy of the states from unnecessary control and undue interference from the centre.

> A key challenge is for the federal system to inculcate and promote the growth of participatory and democratic political culture in the country.

Ethiopian society also exhibits some important unifying factors and obvious potentialities for nation building. The preamble of the Ethiopian federal Constitution refers to the existence of "common interests and the emergence of a common outlook" resulting from centuries-long interactions among the ethnic groups and cultural and religious communities. This seems to be supported by some historical facts. For example, the history of all Ethiopians in defending the sovereignty of the country against colonial aggression at the famous Battle of Adawa in 1896 and other similar cases are cherished and respected symbols of a common legacy. Despite the considerable differences between the various ethnolinguistic groups, the two main religions – Orthodox Christianity (50 percent of the population) and Islam (40 percent of the population) – have served as unifying factors cutting across ethno-linguistic boundaries.

In the globalizing world, national strategies are needed for national survival. Many believe there can be no better option than federal democracy for countries like Ethiopia, which seek to promote national unity without undermining the values and interests of its constituent units. Such legacies and common interests in Ethiopia serve as a basis for its federal system. Indeed, Ethiopia's federal arrangement could be a source of inspiration for others given its geo-political and historical importance and population.

Germany:
The Growth of Social and Economic
Diversity in a Unitary Federal System

PETRA BENDEL / ROLAND STURM

Federalism has a long tradition in Germany. The historical roots of German federalism go back to the Holy Roman Empire and still find an echo in the organisation of the Christian churches, civil society, as well as in the persistence of regional identities. However, German society has undergone major changes in the last few decades. The Federal Republic has, after unification with what was until 1989 communist East Germany, a much more asymmetrical economic structure. The differences in the standard of living between one German region and another were minor in the Federal Republic before 1989. All ten West German regions – known as *Länder* – were roughly the same economically. Yet after German reunification in 1990, despite all the aid to the East from the federal government in Berlin, Germany still consists of six poorer eastern *Länder* and ten richer western *Länder*.

Germany's East has retained economic problems inherited from its past such as high unemployment, a lack of investment, weak growth potential, below average numbers of small and medium-sized enterprises, and a constant brain drain of the young and well-educated to the West and abroad. East/West-distinctions are only one element of the new diversity of German society. Germany has also had to learn from scratch the basics of multiculturalism – a sometimes painful process. Debates over "diversity" are about recent immigrants, as opposed to the poorer East Germans or their richer western counterparts. Generations of immigrant workers from many European countries and elsewhere have enriched German society, but for decades have found few political incentives to integrate.

Today many ethnic minorities live in Germany, the largest being the Turkish minority, with more than 2.4 million of Turkish ancestry living in Germany in 2008 (just slightly more than 1.7 million of these have Turkish citizenship). But there is also a migration by "ethnic Germans" mostly from Russia or other parts of the former Soviet Union. Most immigrants move to where the jobs are, which means to the more prosperous western *Länder*.

Immigration is closely connected with questions of identity. Germany has long based its definition of nationality on ancestry rather than place of birth, to distinguish between "us" and "them" until a reform of the Nationality Act came into effect in 2000. Interior Ministers agreed in 2008 on a national exam that prospective citizens must pass as one of the requirements of citizenship but the German *Länder* still retain some legal authority for determining naturalization prerequisites. At least 90 percent of naturalizations take place in the ten more prosperous western *Länder*.

While the German *Länder* can provide a framework for the integration of immigrants, the implementation of more detailed measurements is the duty of local authorities. In this context the control of education by the *Länder* is very important; their school and educational systems need to be improved in order to offer equal opportunities for immigrants. This is particularly important in eastern Germany since it suffers strongly from emigration and demographic regression.

Migration also has consequences for the social and religious diversity of Germany. Migrants make up an above average share of the unemployed, low achievers in schools, and the socially excluded. Christian migrants have so far not contributed to religious tensions and, with regard to their religion, are not very visible in German society. Muslim traditions or traditions related with Islamic countries, however, have provoked debates in society on the relationship between churches and the state, religious education, co-education, the wearing of religious headscarves and the building of mosques. Most of these are competences of the German *Länder*. It is possible to have religious instruction in German schools but as of mid-2008 there was not a single united Muslim community with whom the *Länder* governments could work to provide Muslim religious instruction.

Completely forgotten in the media and elsewhere in German public discourse are those who have been territorial minorities in Germany for more than a century and are now fully integrated: the Danes in

Schleswig-Holstein, the Sorbians in Saxony and Brandenburg, and the Frieslanders in Lower Saxony and also in Schleswig-Holstein. They are officially recognized minorities who have a guarantee of their cultural heritage. On the other hand, there are still no national minority rights for the 70,000 Sinti and Roma who also form a historically developed minority in Germany; German federalism provides protection for historic territorial minorities only.

This does not mean, however, that federalism is meaningless for other minorities. The *Länder* have the responsibility for public administration, for schools and the curricula. So the questions of religious education, strategies to cope with multicultural backgrounds of students, and the administration of immigration legislation are the responsibility of the *Länder*. Many impulses for such policies come from the local level.

The *Länder* also accept some responsibility for the economic development of their territories. Research shows, however, that the ability of the *Länder* to influence economic data is limited. In the west of Germany a banana-shaped growth region extends from south to north. In the east the official policy is now to concentrate financial aid within clusters of economic growth, irrespective of *Land* borders.

German federalism lacks the flexibility that would make it possible for each *Land* to develop strategies for the new challenges of diversity. Some of this flexibility can be found on the local level, where, for example, innovative initiatives are used to integrate ethnic minorities or to solve the problems of religious education for Muslims. This does not mean that the *Länder* are passive. Their policies are, for the most part, fully integrated in the interconnected decision-making system run by civil servants of the federal government and the *Länder*. Though the Federal Constitutional Court has now developed an interpretation of federalism which supports *Länder* rights more than ever before, the *Länder* still prefer cooperation and are sceptical about too much autonomy. By giving the *Länder* greater competences, the new Federal Reform Act has furthered the disparity among them – especially in the educational system – and eroded their willingness to coordinate policies. So for Germany the debate on unity and diversity is less a debate about two alternatives for federalism, but more about the juxtaposition of federalism and social change.

> So for Germany the debate on unity and diversity is less a debate about two alternatives for federalism, but more about the juxtaposition of federalism and social change.

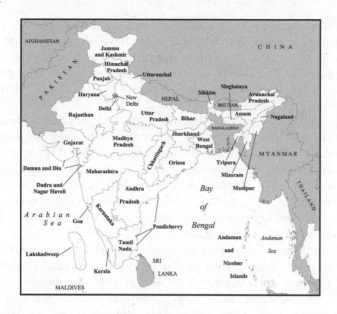

India:
Diversity Unleashed and Federalised

BALVEER ARORA

The year was 1946. India's approach to its diversity was being passionately debated in its newly created Constituent Assembly, which was drawing territories into a new federal democracy. In the years previous, Mahatma Gandhi had mobilized a mass movement – termed nothing more than a "geographic expression" by Winston Churchill – through his non-violent strategies. Crafting a new union was now the task at hand, and it meant grappling with India's age-old linguistic, cultural, and religious diversities. Initially there was a reluctance to recognize diversity as an ordering principle, born of a fear of "excessive federalism." The assertion and consolidation of movements with strong regional roots eventually brought diversity centre-stage, compelling leaders to rethink the foundations of India's unity.

The full force of linguistic and cultural diversities began to be felt in the early years of the Republic. The demand for the linguistic reorganisation of independent India was accompanied by an equally vigorous push for a common language to serve as a *lingua franca* for the Union. At a time when predictions of imminent disintegration and collapse of the Union were rife, political adjustments, mediated by the electoral process, saved the day.

The official language issue was resolved by a compromise which retained English indefinitely as a link language. The 14 states created in 1956 have grown to 28 today, and the 14 languages recognised by the Constitution have increased to 22. Diversity ceased to frighten; it had been federalized. The fear of federalism also gradually diminished as a strong Centre conso-lidated itself.

Despite its extraordinary lengthy detailing of many issues, the Constitution remained ambiguous and ambivalent when it came to the organisation of diversity. While it firmly endorsed the respect of diversity in the chapter on rights, it stopped short of detailing its institutional articu-lation in terms of federal structuring. It conferred the power to recognize diversity on the Union, but left it to the states to manage its socio-political consequences. Two key principles characterised India's approach to diver-sity: asymmetry and accommodation.

Not all ethnic identity related issues were resolved with ease and amicably settled, and many antagonisms persist. They concern mainly the frontier states of Kashmir and Nagaland, as well as the neighbouring states of Mizoram and Manipur. Resorting to asymmetrical federalism helped attenuate tensions in some cases, while special status provisions and generous financial concessions and incentives were also deployed to faci-litate integration in the more intractable cases. The search for solutions was essentially a search for adjustments that could be made on both sides. For the Union, its sovereignty and integrity was paramount, and all solu-tions were worthy of being considered subject to this proviso. For the autonomy movements, the path of negotiations was open provided they did not seek militant secession.

Over the last two decades, the federalization of the party system has thrown up new challenges for governance, even as it gave more space to voice diversity. Regional political parties have succeeded in capturing power in many states, and their contribution to the consolidation of federal democracy is noteworthy. The consolidation of federal coalitions and the *de facto* emergence of proportional representation have given new strength to the unity in diversity principle.

While long established socio-cultural diversities still persist, they seem less threatening today than the growing income disparities generated by rapid growth of certain regions and sectors of economic activity. The crisis of agriculture in several states and related food security issues pose a new set of challenges and tensions under economic liberalisation. Vertical and horizontal fiscal transfers appear to be engaged in a constant race to contain emerging cleavages and disparities. Threats to internal unity due to strains on social harmony and cohesion are seen as new challenges for the federal polity.

What challenges for governance does the persistence of the caste system pose? The dream of a caste-less society seems as elusive as that of a class-less society, partly because both are so closely linked. An intricate system of quotas and reservations in various sectors, designed to promote a more egalitarian society has not produced any significant threats for unity, although they continue to generate political tensions and disorder. In addition to the earlier quotas for scheduled castes and tribes, a new quota for other backward castes in educational institutions and government employment has been legislated.

While it is relatively easy to detail India's diversity, it is far more difficult to explain the many ways in which its unity has been constructed and maintained. The solidarities engendered within the political class by six decades of intensely competitive electoral processes are one means by which an underlying order is preserved. Barring militant movements from the extreme-left, most identity-based parties have used their mobilization capabilities to capture power through the ballot. New connective tissues such as the national passion for cricket, the popularity of Bollywood films, and the rapid spread of telecom firms have given pan Indian discourse a new impetus. The contribution of a unified judiciary headed by the Supreme Court, which enjoys high public esteem, is also a reinforcing factor for unity.

India's search for unity in diversity has led it, with the help of a flexible and adaptable Constitution, to experiment with a wide range of devices available in the federalism toolkit. It negotiates and grants asymmetry to constituent units, provided the basic framework of the Constitution is respected. In their negotiations with movements demanding greater autonomy, the recurring practice of central government leaders has been to allow extensive autonomy provided it is in conformity with the Constitution. Diversity has thus been federalized in diverse ways, retaining the essence of the federal principle but displaying remarkable pragmatism in adjusting it to suit Indian realities. This process of adaptation has been built on the bedrock of electoral democracy. Protest movements have gradually metamorphosed into political parties, assured that the election commission would give them a fair chance at the polls. Ancient diversities, celebrated through the ages, have been given a federal shape and form which enable them to survive and prosper.

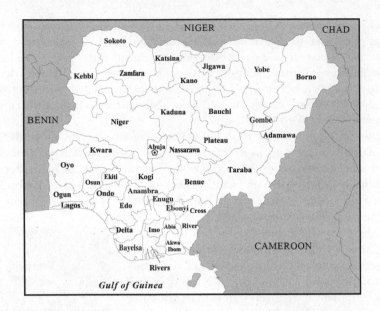

Nigeria: Crafting a Compromise between the Accommodation and Integration of Diversity

ROTIMI T. SUBERU

Nigeria's current constitution of 1999 proclaims the country as "one indivisible and indissoluble nation." Yet, the federation is vexed by multiple sectarian challenges, including pressures for the extension of Islamic *Sharia* law in the Muslim North, a violent insurgency in the oil-bearing southern Niger Delta, internecine struggles between so-called "indigenes" and settlers within the federation's 36 states, and a broad nation-wide clamor for constitutional reform, decentralized federalism, or enhanced recognition of the country's multiple diversities.

Indeed, Nigerian federalism involves a perennial struggle to craft a viable compromise between the promotion of national integration and the accommodation of sectarian identities. The scale of this challenge is evident in the ethnic, regional, and religious fault-lines that fracture Nigeria: a country of 140 million divided into three major ethnic groups (the Muslim Hausa-Fulani in the North, Christian Ibo in the Southeast, and religiously bi-communal Yoruba in the Southwest), hundreds of smaller ethno-linguistic communities (the so-called "ethnic minorities"), and roughly equal numbers of Muslim and Christian adherents. This is overlaid by regional socio-economic disparities and grievances, particularly in the resource-poor, but politically dominant North, and the ecologically and economically neglected Niger Delta.

These cleavages have tested the political ingenuity of Nigeria's successive rulers since the amalgamation of the country's diverse territorial communities by English colonizers in 1914. British colonial policy, for instance, sought explicitly to provide adequately for the country's diversities within a framework of Nigerian unity. This included the establishment of a decentralized three-region federation in 1954 built around Nigeria's major ethnic divisions. But this ethno-regional federalism aggravated sectional inequalities and animosities, leading to the collapse of parliamentary government in the post-independence First Republic lasting from 1960 to 1966, bloody ethno-military coups and conflicts, and an Ibo-based secessionist war occurring between 1967 and 1970.

This turbulence pushed Nigeria's military rulers and their civilian constitutional advisers and successors towards a more centrist or integrationist management of the country's diversities. This policy of national integration and political centralization was entrenched in the 1979, 1989, and 1999 Constitutions that the military, which ruled the country in those periods, bequeathed to the Second, Third, and Fourth Nigerian Republics, respectively. Its major features include: the dissolution of the three large ethnic majority-based regions into smaller and weaker sub-ethnic, multi-ethnic, or minority-ethnic states; the expansion of the legislative powers of the federal government, including the centrali-zation of the revenue sharing, local government, police and judicial systems; the abandonment of the parliamentary model of government for a strong executive presidential system, in which a nationally elected president is expected to function as a putative symbol of pan-Nigerian unity; and the introduction of the so-called "federal character" principle, which mandates the equal representation of the "indigenes" (or ethnic groups which settled the various geographic regions of Nigeria) of the states in the government and public agencies of the federation, including the political parties. It is a form of affirmative action.

These integrative strategies have been remarkably effective in cross-cutting and attenuating sectional identities. They also prevented a recurrence of secessionist warfare and promoted a broad commitment to the idea of Nigerian unity, in-cluding the development by civilian politicians of innovative, but informal schemes for the sharing and rotation of key political offices (particularly the presi-dency) among ethnic, regional, and religious segments of the country. Yet, the strategies have engendered their own contradictions, which were aggravated by the despotic centralism of more recent (1984-1999) northern-led military governments.

Many Nigerians contend that the ethnic, regional, and religious tensions that currently plague the country represent a centrifugal backlash to the excessive centralization of powers and resources under the present system of unitary federalism. They call for the replacement of the current military-facilitated constitutional framework with a democratically or popularly negotiated people's constitution. This would return Nigeria to a modified form of the First Republic's "true federalism," or to a more pluralist accommodation of the country's diversities, including the decentralization of powers and resources to larger and fewer regional or ethnic states.

Yet, the ongoing agitations for major constitutional reforms in Nigeria are stymied by significant inter-regional differences over the precise details or scope of change, which impede the attainment of the concurrent federal-state legislative supermajorities required for amendments to the country's basic law. The predominantly Christian South, for instance, is suspicious of pressures for the accommodation of Islamic law in the Muslim North; the latter, in turn, sees southern demands for fiscal decentralization as contrary to the North's dependence on the effective inter-regional redistribution of resources.

Nigeria can perhaps learn from Canada's sobering experiences with the failure of mega-constitutional politics by pursuing non-constitutional political renewal or intra-constitutional legislative reforms as a pragmatic response to the difficulty of large-scale, fundamental constitutional change. Alternatively, Nigeria can seek political restructuring through the pursuit of incremental – rather than comprehensive – constitutional change, with priority given to such relatively less ethno-politically explosive, but governance-enhancing, issues as corruption control, electoral reform, and the promotion of the rights of women and children.

> Indeed, a fundamental defect of the current practice of national integration and centralization in Nigeria is the failure of the approach to effectively advance political democracy and good economic governance as potentially robust bases for reinforcing Nigeria's unity in diversity.

Indeed, a fundamental defect of the current practice of national integration and centralization in Nigeria is the failure of the approach to effectively advance political democracy and good economic governance as potentially robust bases for reinforcing Nigeria's unity in diversity. Rather, the continuing mismanagement of the country's oil wealth and the massive corruption of its electoral processes have sorely strained Nigeria's federal unity. Specifically, the centralized redistribution of federal oil revenues to sub-federal governments has lacked transparency, serving to enrich a narrow local elite class rather than to alleviate the inter-regional inequalities and the mass poverty that fuel ethno-regional militancy and religious extremism. Similarly, the manipulation of electoral processes by dominant political elites has virtually foisted a single-party hegemony on the entire federation, thereby undermining even the modest political decentralization envisaged under Nigeria's centrist constitution.

Nigeria's current difficulties with federalism and diversity issues are, therefore, intricately linked with broader questions of economic governance and democratization in the country. As the country's rulers continually seek to fashion a sustainable balance between national integration and ethno-religious and regional accommodation, they will also need to creatively reconcile this federalist compromise with the imperatives of democratic development and economic progress.

Minority Rights and the Impact of Authoritarian Regression in Russia's Federalism

IRINA BUSYGINA /
ANDREAS HEINEMANN-GRÜDER

Russia is ethnically and regionally very heterogeneous. Combining both ethno-federalism and territorial federalism, the country's 89 constituent units are divided into six different types: republics, autonomous districts, one autonomous region, territorial regions, districts, and two federal cities. During the 1990s, 32 out of its then 89 constituent units, 85 today, existed as ethnic autonomies – among them 21 republics, ten autonomous districts and the Jewish autonomous region. At the beginning of the 1990s, the republics pioneered federalization in Russia by forming loose coalitions; the then president Boris Yeltsin had addressed the leaders of these republics – mainly Tatarstan and Bashkortostan with the famous phrase: "Take as much sovereignty as you can swallow." This message is a far cry from the de-ethnicization of federalism led by the centre in today's Russia.

Resembling nation-states in several respects, republics help to preserve and develop regional and ethnic identities. Conventional justifications for having been assigned the status of "republic" include traditions of settlement, the spiritual meaning of a given territory ("homeland"), and making amends for past historical grievances. Republics have the power to adopt constitutions and introduce their own state languages. They can also sign international treaties providing they respect the confines of the federal Constitution. With the exception of the Constitution and state languages, most other competencies are shared by the purely territorial entities, the oblasti, and the kraya.

At the time of the last census of 2002, there were 41 titular non-Russian ethnic groups, who individually or together provided the name for a region of the federation; however, in most of the ethnic regions native people are not predominant. All in all, in ten out of 21 republics the titular ethnic group forms the majority, but among the autonomous districts, not a single

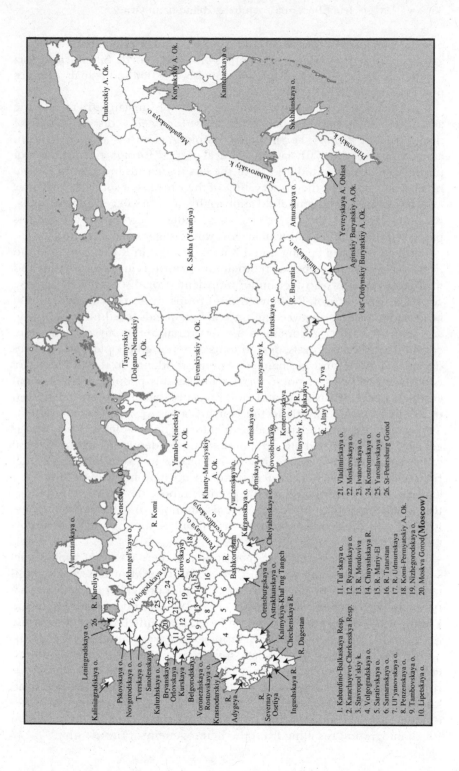

Chukotskiy A. Ok.

Koryakskiy A. Ok.

Kamchatskaya o.

Magadanskaya o.

Sakhalinskaya o.

Khabarovskiy k.

Primorskiy k.

Amurskaya o.

Yevreyskaya A. Oblast

R. Sakha (Yakutiya)

Aginskiy Buryatskiy A.Ok.

Ust'-Ordynskiy Buryatskiy A. Ok.

Chitinskaya o.

R. Buryatia

Taymyrskiy
(Dolgano-Nenetskiy)
A. Ok.

Evenkiyskiy A. Ok.

Irkutskaya o.

Krasnoyarskiy k.

R. Tyva

R. Altay

R. Khakasiya

Kemerovskaya o.

Altayskiy k.

Yamalo-Nenetskiy
A. Ok.

Tomskaya o.

Novosibirskaya o.

Omskaya o.

Khanty-Mansiyskiy
A. Ok.

Tyumenskaya o.

Kurganskaya o.

Chelyabinskaya o.

Sverdlovskaya o.

Permskaya o.

Bashkortostan

R. Komi

Nenetskiy A. Ok.

Arkhangel'skaya o.

Murmanskaya o.

R. Kareliya

Leningradskaya o.

Kaliningradskaya o.

Pskovskaya o.

Novgorodskaya o.

Tverskaya o.

Smolenskaya o.

Kaluzhskaya o.

Bryanskaya o.

Orlovskaya

Kurskaya

Belgorodskaya

Voronezhskaya o.

Rostovskaya o.

Krasnodarskiy k.

R. Adygeya

R. Severnay Osetiya

Ingushskaya R.

R. Dagestan

Chechenskaya R.

Kalmykiya-Khal'mg Tangch

Astrakhanskaya o.

Orenburgskaya o.

Vologodskaya o.

Kirovskaya

- 1. Kabardino-Balkaskaya Resp.
- 2. Karachayevo-Cherkesskaya Resp.
- 3. Stavropol'skiy k.
- 4. Volgogradskaya o.
- 5. Sarativskaya o.
- 6. Samarskaya o.
- 7. Ul'yanovskaya o.
- 8. Penzenskaya o.
- 9. Tambovskaya o.
- 10. Lipetskaya o.

- 11. Tul'skaya o.
- 12. Ryazanskaya o.
- 13. R. Mordoviya
- 14. Chuvashskaya R.
- 15. R. Mariy-El
- 16. R. Tatarstan
- 17. R. Udmurtskaya
- 18. Komi-Permyatskiy A. Ok.
- 19. Nizhegorodskaya o.
- 20. Moskva Gorod(**Moscow**)

- 21. Vladimirskaya o.
- 22. Moskovskaya o.
- 23. Ivanovskaya o.
- 24. Kostromskaya o.
- 25. Yaroslavskaya o.
- 26. St-Petersburg Gorod

one has a majority of the titular ethnic group. Smaller populations of ethnic groups include the indigenous peoples of the far North, Siberia, and Asia – officially 45 registered peoples of roughly 275,000 individuals who are distributed over 27 regions.

Contradictions between the formal equality of Russian citizens and the actual implementation of laws often allow for *de facto* discrimination of non-dominant groups. For instance, ethnic groups are allowed to form associations, yet the 2001 "law on political parties" forbids the formation of parties on ethnic grounds. Some of the less numerous indigenous people receive assistance for the preservation of their means of survival. They may also be granted preferential taxation rights and privileged use of public property. However the *de facto* rights of indigenous people are far less protected than the list of formal rights would suggest.

Conflicts with and among non-dominant groups in Russia can be found in various forms: those between titular ethnic groups in ethnic regions and non-titular groups who feel under-represented or discriminated against; conflicts between non-Russian ethnic groups over the ethno-territorial boundaries inside or between autonomies; demands by ethnic groups who are part of existing autonomies for territorial autonomy of their own; conflicts between migrants, descendents of deported people, and refugees on the one hand and permanent regional residents on the other; socio-economic problems of non-populous indigenous peoples; intra-regional conflicts between Russians and non-Russians that led to an emigration of ethnic Russians (mostly in the North Caucasus); and violent conflicts with nationalist or fundamentalist militants. The conflict in Chechnya is certainly the most striking evidence of the inadequacies of the federal policy towards non-dominant groups: its inability to institutionalize conflict regulation, the rejection of negotiations with nationalist opposition, the excessive emergency powers of the president, poor development impulses, the inefficiency of inter-regional redistribution, and the unwillingness to cope with the repression under Stalinism, are among the most important deficits.

Whereas Soviet federalism was perceived as a mere means of symbolically solving the "nationality problem," the re-foundation of Russia was originally characterized by the exporting of federal principles into state construction. With the end of the Yeltsin era in 1999, and the beginning of the Putin period, the prevailing views on federalism shifted. In order to justify his centralizing agenda, Putin's supporters have pointed to deficits in Yeltsin's federal system such as: sovereignty claims of the republics, contradictions between the Russian Constitution and the constitutions of the republics, hierarchy among regions, language legislation favouring languages other than Russian, problems of inter-governmental coordination, the alleged weakening of state capacity, as well as the potential for disintegration resulting from the heterogeneity of the country.

After a phase of ethnicization of federalism, the second half of the 1990s has produced a phase of de-ethnicization; economic and political expectations have superseded ethnic calculations. The de-ethnicization of federalism corresponds with a so-called "russification" of the state in the sense of an explicit and implicit preference for the attributes of the Russian dominant culture *vis-à-vis* non-Russian cultures. There has been no official farewell to federalism; the disempowerment of the regions is depicted instead as a strengthening of federalism. There has been a profound shift in the federal attitude towards republics. While during the 1990s they were treated as a special type of constituent entity, today the centre's relationship with the purely territorial and ethnic regions is mostly symmetrical.

> In formal institutional terms, Russia is no longer a federation. The sources of Russian federalism are nonetheless deeper than Putin's instrumentalism seem to suggest.

The official conception of federalism has to some extent made a return to its Soviet past. Regions are treated as mere parts of the intergovernmental, administrative-territorial machinery. The imposition of uniform rules under Putin's presidency has led to neither a strengthening of the rule of law and of checks and balances nor has it curbed the authoritarian policy styles of governors or republican presidents. Rather, it has undermined the prerequisites for democratization. De-federalization and de-democratization have gone hand-in-hand.

The radical reduction of accessibility or institutionalized participatory rights *vis-à-vis* the central government has led to non-transparent, informal ways of pursuing one's interests, including a policy of favors. The political infighting over the institutional structure and division of competencies is still not resolved. In formal institutional terms, Russia is no longer a federation. The sources of Russian federalism are nonetheless deeper than Putin's instrumentalism seem to suggest. Putin's centralism, institutionally unstable and characterized by a disrespect for constitutional principles, repeats the mistake of the defunct Soviet system. It is systematically overburdened, unable to learn from its errors, extremely personalized, and displays a low degree of predictability.

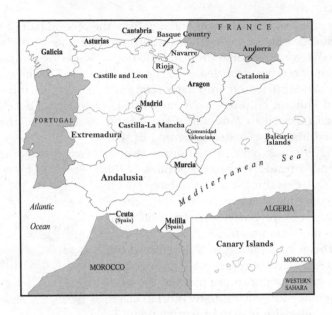

Diversity and Unity in Spain's
Estado De Las Autonomías

CÉSAR COLINO / LUIS MORENO

Some countries face a national question. Spain has rather a question of nationalities and regions. Despite ongoing tensions in the functioning of its political structure, secessionist aspirations of some of its citizens, and diversity in language, socioeconomic status, and territorial identities, the case of Spain can serve as a model for other diverse countries facing similar challenges for accommodating long-standing diversity and unity.

Spain was established as the first modern state in Europe by means of a dynastic union of the Catholic monarchy in the second half of the 15th century. However, its constituent territories maintained their political existence. In the following centuries there were failed attempts at constituting a centralized polity along the lines of the French model. This failure was reflected in the emergence in 19th and 20th centuries of different local regionalisms and nationalisms claiming autonomy, home rule, or even secession. Efforts to accommodate them in the short-lived First Federal Republic (1873) and the Second Republic (1931-1939) failed. After the demise of General Franco's dictatorship (1939-1975) a wide social and political consensus was achieved with the 1978 Constitution.

The 1978 Constitution initiated a deep process of political and administrative decentralization that took place in parallel with that of democratization.

The democratic constitution opted for an open-ended model of territorial organization of a federalizing nature and established a "State of autonomous communities" or *Estado de las Autonomías*. Although the "f" word does not appear in the Constitution, it established provisions devised to accommodate a diversity of collective identities within Spain, as well as to address historical grievances and articulate a long-standing inclination for regional self-rule. The process of devolution of administrative and political powers started in the early 1980s in three territories that had previous experience with autonomy and a constitutionally recognized vernacular language in addition to the state-wide official Spanish (or *castellano*). These three territories – the Basque Country, Catalonia, and Galicia – are usually known as "historical nationalities." Soon after a second group of regions, Andalusia, Canary Islands, Navarre, and Valencia, mobilized in order to achieve the same powers of self-rule as those of the historical nationalities. Since then, all 17 nationalities and regions have engaged in a multiple horizontal competition for power and resources, some of them in order to maintain a special status and some to remain on the same footing as the others.

> Although the "f" word does not appear in the Constitution, it established provisions devised to accommodate a diversity of collective identities within Spain, as well as to address historical grievances and articulate a long-standing inclination for regional self-rule.

The 1978 Constitution also sanctioned various asymmetries, among which the recognition and protection of a quasi independent fiscal regime in the Basque Country and Navarre, and a special economic-fiscal regime for the Canary Islands, should be underlined. Traditional civil law systems in Catalonia, Galicia, Navarre, Valencia, Balearic Islands, Aragon, and Basque Country were also recognized.

The functioning of the state has been underpinned by two main tensions. The first is a vertical tension between regional governments and the central government. The former have often sought after more powers and resources from the centre; the latter has strived to keep its policy-making role state-wide. Second, a horizontal tension exists among the autonomous communities themselves. Some have attempted to maintain a different status from the rest of the regions, while others have aimed to achieve the same institutional and political resources. These tensions have manifested in the evolution of the party system, with a relevant presence of local nationalist parties in some autonomous communities. Some of these parties advocate confederal or secessionist options, while others declare loyalty to the existing model of federal-like statehood, although they also claim a deeper degree of regional autonomy. In other *Comunidades Autónomas*, local nationalism is confronted by different versions of Spanish state-nationalism with strong ideas of equality, cohesion, and unity.

A minority of citizens in the Basque Country, Catalonia, and Galicia aspire to outright independence. In the Basque Country, some of them support the ideas of ETA, a Basque acronym for "Basque Homeland and Freedom," a terrorist group advocating secession with Navarre and the French Basque Country. In the whole of Spain, however, more than two-thirds of its citizens express a dual identity or compound nationality. This dual identity incorporates both regional and state-wide identities in various degrees and without apparent contradiction between them. Such a dual identity is at the root of the federalizing rationale of the *Estado de las Autonomías,* which has largely transcended previous patterns of internal confrontation.

Spain's linguistic diversity is at the base of many political claims put forward by local nationalisms. These language differences are often politicized in order to request a greater degree of autonomy in the running of policy areas such as education, health, planning, or social services, now fully devolved to the *Comunidades Autónomas.* Unlike the cases of Switzerland, Canada, or Belgium, in those Spanish regions with official local languages, virtually everyone can speak – and be understood – in Spanish. Some political parties and civil society groups have proposed the use of co-official local languages in nationwide institutions, to the detriment of the common language, as a way of recognizing diversity. For others, it seems unreasonable to renounce the use of a common and world language like *castellano* Spanish.

Spain is also socio-economically diverse. A majority of citizens (57.8 percent of the Spanish population) live in four *Comunidades Autónomas:* Andalusia, Catalonia, Madrid, and Valencia. The regional share of gross domestic product (GDP) by these four *Comunidades Autónomas* represents 59.9 percent of the total. Likewise, ten regions have a population of less than five percent of the total, and ten regions account for less than five per cent of GDP. Concerning religion, a majority of Spaniards profess to be Roman Catholics, including the majority of Basque and Catalan nationalists. The North African cities of Ceuta and Melilla now have large Islamic minorities. At present, Spain has around 4.5 million immigrants (ten percent of the total population), mainly from Latin American countries and Morocco, who work mainly in Catalonia, the Mediterranean coast, and Madrid. Changes in the demographic structure are bound to result in new political and constitutional tensions.

Through pacts at the political level and the successful accommodation of a diversity of interests through negotiation, Spain has had a relatively smooth transition to democracy since the late 1970s. Accommodation of regional interests in policy making has also been accomplished through intergovernmental relations among the national government and autonomous communities – mostly through ministerial sectoral conferences and, more recently, through the Prime Ministers' Conference. Internal negotiation of divergences within parties and other informal practices, such as building the Spanish cabinet with ministers coming from different regions, have also played an important role in accommodating regional interests. However, a main shortcoming of "federal" Spain is represented by the dysfunctional workings of the Senate – many Spaniards consider it a constitutionally ill-defined chamber of territorial representation.

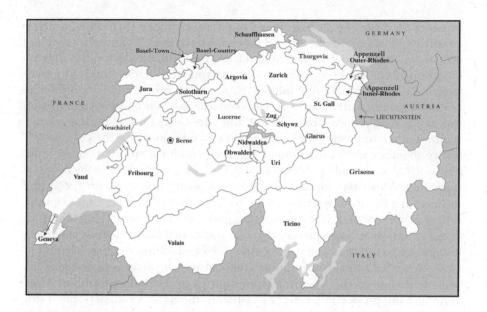

Switzerland:
Success with Traditional Minorities,
Challenges with New Immigrants

THOMAS FLEINER / MAYA HERTIG RANDALL

In his humorous depiction of Switzerland called "Switzerland for Beginners," author George Mikes describes the Swiss Confederation as the biggest country in the world. He is referring to the Swiss phenomenon of moving to a neighbouring canton feeling like a move to another country. There is often a different language spoken, a different religion practiced, and a different culture in place. Put differently, despite a territory of only 41,290 km – less than a tenth of the size of Spain – Switzerland is a big country in terms of diversity.

The Swiss Federation was created in 1848 after a religiously motivated civil war, uniting 26 cantons, 2715 municipalities, four national languages: German (spoken by 64 percent), French (20 percent), Italian (6.5 percent), and Romansch (0.5 percent), as well as two major religions: Roman Catholicism (practiced by 42 percent) and Protestantism (33 percent), not to mention the tiny minority of Jewish and Old Catholic creeds. With 20 percent of the population, foreign nationals further enhance Switzerland's diversity.

In contrast to ethnic federations, such as Belgium, linguistic, religious, cultural, and economic boundaries generally do not coincide in Switzerland;

however the resulting cleavages tend to counterbalance each other, which is conducive to internal cohesion and stability. Switzerland distinguishes itself not only from ethnic federations but also from traditional nation states that are based on either the French or the German model of nationhood. The Swiss nation is known as "nation of will" or "nation by choice" and is conceived of as neither a unitary, indivisible entity based on a civic identity (the French model) nor as a homogeneous ethno-cultural unit (the German model). It is conceptualized as a composite nation, based on shared values and the citizens' will to live together within one state. Every Swiss national simultaneously holds a municipal, cantonal, and federal citizenship, each of which reflects one of three complementary identities. The Swiss Constitution explicitly recognizes diversity as a foundational value that is to be promoted, considering linguistic, religious, and cultural differences an integral part of an overarching Swiss political identity. As a consequence, the four traditional languages are all equally recognized as national languages of the Swiss Federation despite their numerical strength. Other constitutional and statutory provisions provide for fair representation of the linguistic communities in federal institutions. More generally, the proportional election system to the Swiss National Council (the chamber of Parliament representing the people), the egalitarian representation of the cantons in the second chamber (the Council of States), as well as power sharing and a consensus-driven political culture marked by self restraint, ensure that smaller communities are not outvoted. For instance, since 1959 the four major political parties represented in the federal parliament have shared power in the Federal Council and decisions are generally made by consensus.

Power sharing and the quest for consensus have been greatly favoured by direct democracy, used frequently on all three levels of government and constituting an essential element of Swiss national identity. At the federal order, the popular initiative enables minorities to gain political influence by proposing a constitutional amendment and submitting it to a vote. Via the referendum, the citizens have the right to approve or reject federal statutes, international treaties, and constitutional amendments. The instruments of direct democracy also act as a safeguard against excessive centralization and guarantee the cantons a large degree of autonomy. At the cantonal order, they protect the substantive autonomy of the municipalities. The emphasis on collective autonomy of local communities rather than individual liberties is another typical feature of Swiss Federalism. Freedom is mainly understood in democratic and participatory terms. As much as possible, decisions are made at the level closest to the people in order to enhance individual voice. Federalism is thus understood as a prerequisite of democracy and not as an opposing principle. It is the key for a polity close to its citizens and governed by consent. A large amount of political, financial, and organizational autonomy is the main institutional and political means to accommodating Switzerland's diversity. This autonomy is the essential element of cantonal sovereignty, which is explicitly recognized in the federal Constitution, and also guarantees that meaningful powers can be exercised at the municipal order. By granting local autonomy to cantons and municipalities, Switzerland ensures that different cultures are not ignored or confined to the private sphere.

The positive side of local autonomy is that it provides a homeland and a special identity for citizens and guarantees the right to be different. Based on their autonomy, cantons and, in many cases municipalities, decide on their official language for the administration, courts, and schools. They also define – within the limits of individual religious freedom – their relationship with the traditional churches, which leaves room for many different options. While some cantons recognize an official church, others follow a model of strict religious neutrality, based on the clear separation between church and state. Cantons, and sometimes even municipalities, have different religious holidays depending on the majority of their populations and their historical religious backgrounds. They are, moreover, free to grant their religious communities collective autonomy. Generally an asset for a multicultural federation, local autonomy empowers local democracies to develop their institutional, economic, and political solutions appropriate to their needs and interests. Moreover, local autonomy induces both competition among various polities and policy innovation.

> Federalism is thus understood as a prerequisite of democracy and not as an opposing principle. It is the key for a polity close to its citizens and governed by consent. A large amount of political, financial, and organizational autonomy is the main institutional and political means to accommodating Switzerland's diversity.

Nevertheless, the fragmented Swiss polity confronts many problems. The roots of Switzerland's diversity are mainly historical and concentrated in clearly defined territories. Currently, Switzerland needs to face up to the challenge of a new influx of diversity caused by modern migration, which lacks a clear territorial basis. How can foreign nationals be integrated within the Swiss concept of a "nation of will" composed of traditional diversities with an accommodation strategy heavily based on territorial autonomy? Another challenge to Switzerland's diversity is the strong impact and standardizing pressure emanating from the global and the European markets. A democracy such as Switzerland risks paralysis from parochialism. The tendency is to reject new diversities, adopting a policy of differential exclusion in order to insulate against outside influence. Switzerland's rejection of European Union membership is a case in point. Moreover, the mechanisms of direct democracy, which have played a crucial role in accommodating traditional diversities, tend to be used by right-wing, populist parties as a vehicle for discriminatory and xenophobic policies. Today's complexities require quick, efficient, and often costly solutions. Switzerland will only be able to uphold its unity in diversity by its federal and democratic structure. Thus it will have to find the way to cope with future fundamental challenges by adapting, developing, and modernizing federalism without undermining it.

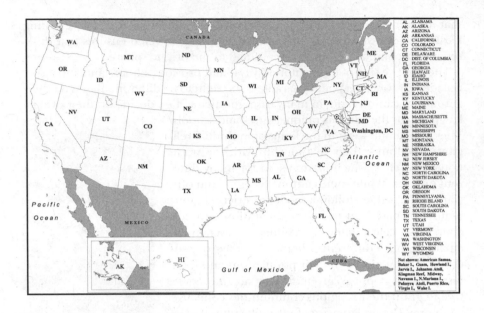

AL ALABAMA
AK ALASKA
AZ ARIZONA
AR ARKANSAS
CA CALIFORNIA
CO COLORADO
CT CONNECTICUT
DE DELAWARE
DC DIST. OF COLUMBIA
FL FLORIDA
GA GEORGIA
HI HAWAII
ID IDAHO
IL ILLINOIS
IN INDIANA
IA IOWA
KS KANSAS
KY KENTUCKY
LA LOUISIANA
ME MAINE
MD MARYLAND
MA MASSACHUSETTS
MI MICHIGAN
MN MINNESOTA
MS MISSISSIPPI
MO MISSOURI
MT MONTANA
NE NEBRASKA
NV NEVADA
NH NEW HAMPSHIRE
NJ NEW JERSEY
NM NEW MEXICO
NY NEW YORK
NC NORTH CAROLINA
ND NORTH DAKOTA
OH OHIO
OK OKLAHOMA
OR OREGON
PA PENNSYLVANIA
RI RHODE ISLAND
SC SOUTH CAROLINA
SD SOUTH DAKOTA
TN TENNESSEE
TX TEXAS
UT UTAH
VT VERMONT
VA VIRGINIA
WA WASHINGTON
WV WEST VIRGINIA
WI WISCONSIN
WY WYOMING

Not shown: American Samoa,
Baker I., Guam, Howland I.,
Jarvis I., Johnston Atoll,
Kingman Reef, Midway,
Navassa I., N.Mariana I.,
Palmyra Atoll, Puerto Rico,
Virgin I., Wake I.

The United States of America: Multiculturalism without Federalism

JOHN KINCAID

The United States is one of the world's most diverse countries. Virtually every race, nationality, tribe, ethnic group, language, religion, and culture present in the world exists in the United States. Being the world's third largest nation in land area (9.83 million square kilometers) and population (304 million), the United States is geographically and socio-economically diverse, with considerable life-style diversity too. Yet, American federalism is remarkably homogeneous and hostile to ethnic- or linguistic-based territories. Instead, cultural diversity (except for the cultures of America's Aboriginal peoples, commonly referred to as "Indians" or "Native Americans") finds its expression primarily in the private sector, for which governments provide rights guarantees.

The founders of the United States invented modern federalism, but not with the intention of accommodating cultural communities seeking to create territorially based "homelands." The United States is a nation of immigrants. No one, except descendents of the original Indian inhabitants, can claim any ancestral homeland, nor has any immigrant group successfully claimed, like Quebecers in Canada, to be a distinct society entitled to occupy and rule a constituent state in perpetuity. Instead, territory is neutral. Only constitutionally and legally recognized geographic jurisdictions (i.e., states and localities), not the communities of people within them, are potentially perpetual.

The U.S. Constitution guarantees everyone free entry into and exit from all jurisdictions (except for some Indian lands) because the founders desired, foremost, to protect individual liberty and promote commercial prosperity. The control of any jurisdiction belongs to the majority that occupies the territory at any point in time. Given high levels of population mobility, majorities in most states and localities are fluid. For example, as the population composition of Los Angeles changed during the late 20th century, white mayors were replaced by black mayors and then by Latino mayors.

The creation of the federal system during the 1780s did, however, partly reflect a need to accommodate territorially entrenched geographic, socio-economic, and cultural diversities in the 13 original states. Most critical was the divide between the northern and southern states created by the existence of African slavery in the South. Even though white northerners and southerners shared the same language, religions, Anglo and northern European cultural heritages, and basic political principles, the southern "slavocracy" generated a distinct culture that gave rise, in effect, to a separate nation. In this respect, the United States came into being as two nations in one country – a *de facto* bicommunal federation – even though the Constitution is, arguably, against such a division. This *de facto* division sustained non-centralized federalism by asserting states' rights and limiting exercises of federal powers. However, the union experienced conflicts and instabilities often characteristic of bicommunal countries, including a horrific civil war from 1861 to 1865. John C. Calhoun, a U.S. Vice President and U.S. Senator from South Carolina, had tried to save the union by proposing amendments, such as concurrent-majority rule and a dual (North-South) presidency, which would have turned the Constitution into a union of two territories. But such a union, along with slavery, was anathema to most northerners.

At first, the South's defeat in the Civil War seemed to destroy slavery and the existence of two sovereign territories. Indeed, hostility to any territories based on religion, belief, or ethnicity was reflected after the war in the federal government's military war against the western Indians and legal war against polygamy in Mormon Utah. Both wars ended with federal victories in the early 1890s. Assimilation of Indians, Mormons, and millions of immigrants into an American "melting pot" was a corollary post-war response to ethnic diversity. As a result, federal power increased and, at times, degraded state powers. However, after federal troops withdrew from the South during the early 1870s, a *de facto* division of the United States was resurrected by southern white supremacists who, along with some northern white conservatives, defended states' rights again and opposed expansive federal power. Even during the New Deal of the 1930s when the federal government vastly increased its power over the economy, states' rights advocates blocked most federal threats to state powers important to them. In the early 1960s the black civil rights movement compelled massive federal-government intervention, including military intervention, into state and local affairs, putting an end to the North-South division.

This produced an exponential increase in federal power over the states and their local governments. Today, no territorially based political force has a sustained interest in asserting states' rights against federal power.

Subsequent liberation movements (e.g., women, Indians, Latinos, Asians, gays, and disabled people) also entreated the federal government to protect their rights. Other movements, such as environmentalism, argued that social problems spill across state and local boundaries, thus requiring federal intervention. Thorough nationalization and initial globalization of the U.S. eco-nomy led to calls for more federal regulation to override state and local regulatory barriers to intra-national commerce. In turn, political parties became more national in their organization and operation.

These liberation movements proposed multiculturalism as an alternative to what they believed was a historically racist, sexist, and homophobic melting pot. They demanded governmental and societal recognition of their identities; proportional representation in federal, state, and local government institutions, plus government guarantees of their rights; protections against discrimination; equalizing affirmative-action, comparable-worth, accessibility, and social-welfare policies; and public services such as multilingual education and ballots to meet language needs. Yet only Indians today assert ancestral land claims and call themselves a "nation."

> Multiculturalism has been associated with a flowering of federalism in many parts of the world. In the United States, however, multiculturalism has been associated with a weakening or even dissolution of federalism.

Another expression of multiculturalism was reform of federal laws in 1968 to admit more immigrants and abolish preferences for European immigrants. This reform produced massive increases of immigration from Latin America, Asia, Africa, and the Middle East. Foreign-born residents increased from 4.7 percent of the U.S. population in 1970 to 12.5 percent (totaling 37.5 million people) by 2006. Although immigrants retain many elements of their cultures, including language, most immigrants also pursue assimilation.

Multiculturalism has been associated with a flowering of federalism in many parts of the world. In the United States, however, multiculturalism has been associated with a weakening or even dissolution of federalism. This is so because American multiculturalism has no constitutional or legal bases for establishing territorial expressions that could demand federalist accommodations. On the contrary, contemporary multiculturalism is the product of a massive liberation of persons from the tyranny of states and small towns, a liberation fostered by a vast expansion of federal power over state and local governments. Those governments continue to play important roles, but diversity is protected predominantly by federal legal and social policies. Thus, whatever the future of American diversity, it will not likely include non-centralized federalism in which the states function as vigorously autonomous self-governing polities.

Glossary

ABORIGINALS 1. original inhabitants of a country or territory; replaces the expression Indians in Canada (though not in USA); also Aboriginal peoples; indigenous peoples, native peoples. 2. Original inhabitants of Australia; replaces Aborigines.

ABORIGINAL LAND RIGHTS rights of possession accorded to aboriginal peoples in Australia and elsewhere despite their lack of formal ownership.

ABORIGINES standard term until recently for the Aboriginal people of Australia.

AFFIRMATIVE ACTION policy of systematically favouring disadvantaged groups in access or employment, services and other benefits.

ASSIMILATION absorption of different ethnic, racial or cultural groups into the dominant culture.

ASYMMETRICAL FEDERALISM unequal or non-identical distribution of powers and responsibilities between the constituent units of a federal system; e.g. the greater autonomy accorded the Basque Country, Catalonia and Navarre than the other Autonomous Communities in Spain.

AUTONOMOUS DISTRICTS self-governing regions within OBLASTI (provinces) of the Russian federation.

CANTON name of the 26 constituent units of the Swiss federation.

CASTE SYSTEM traditional system of social stratification in India.

COMMONWEALTH GOVERNMENT central government of the 'Commonwealth of Australia'.

COMMUNITIES non-territorial divisions of the Belgian federation.

CONCURRENT POWERS responsibilities that are assigned to one order of government in a federation without being made exclusive; shared powers.

CONFEDERALISM decentralised form of union where sovereignty and most powers reside with the constituent units and the central government has little direct relationship with the people.

CONSTITUENT UNITS the constitutionally guaranteed territorial units of which a federation is composed – STATES, PROVINCES, CANTONS, *LÄNDER*, etc.

COOPERATIVE FEDERALISM the practice and principle of modern federalism whereby the levels of government work together to coordinate policy design and delivery; does not necessarily entail an equality of power and resources between the two sides.

COUNCIL OF STATES second chamber of the Swiss parliament, in principle representing the cantons.

CROWN the executive authority of the Westminster system of government as practised in Australia and Canada.

DIRECT DEMOCRACY democratic processes whereby citizens participate in decision making without representatives acting for them.

DISTRICTS administrative zones of the government of the Russian federation.

EQUALIZATION formal redistribution of revenues across a federation to provide a minimum standard of resourcing for jurisdictions regardless of their fiscal capacity and thereby ensure citizens a comparable level of government services regardless of their place of residence; technically known as 'horizontal fiscal equalization' (HFE). Typically based on a 'formula' that takes into account either or both the own-source revenue capacity or/and the expenditure requirements (needs) of the different jurisdictions.

EXECUTIVE FEDERALISM process of intergovernmental agreement-making between the executive branches of the two levels of government in a federation, with limited or no participation by the legislative branches.

FEDERAL CONSTITUTIONAL COURT *Bundesverfassungsgericht;* the specialist judicial body for matters of constitutional law in Germany.

FEDERAL COUNCIL collegial executive body of the Swiss government.

FEDERAL REFORM ACT suite of constitutional amendments passed in 2006 to rationalise the division of powers and responsibilities in the German federal system and reduce the range of matters on which the *Bundesrat,* or Federal Council, carries a veto.

FEDERAL SOCIETY regional or territorially-based diversity underlying a federal structure.

FIRST NATIONS original inhabitants of North America; see ABORIGINALS.

FISCAL IMBALANCE an imbalance in revenues and responsibilities between the levels of government in a federation, with one level enjoying revenues in excess of its needs and the other or others bearing expenditure responsibilities in excess of their own-source revenues; also known 'fiscal gap' or 'vertical fiscal imbalance' (VFI).

HORIZONTAL FISCAL TRANSFERS See EQUALIZATION.

HOUSE OF FEDERATION second chamber of the Ethiopian federation; Council of the Federation.

INDIANS traditional designation of ABORIGINAL PEOPLES of sub-Arctic North America.

INDIGENOUS PEOPLES See ABORIGINALS.

INUIT native inhabitants of the Arctic; see ABORIGINAL PEOPLES.

KRAYA one category comprising 9 of the 83 constituent units of the Russian federation, largely equivalent to OBLASTI and distinguished primarily by the historical significance of their geographic location (frontier); translates as 'Territories'.

LÄNDER   (singular: *Land*) term for the constituent units of the German and Austrian federations; equivalent to States or provinces.

MELTING POT   traditional metaphor to characterise the absorption or assimilation of diverse cultures into the dominant culture of the United States.

MERCOSUR   regional trade agreement linking Argentina, Brazil, Paraguay, Uruguay and Venezuela; *Mercado Común del Sur* (Southern Common Market).

MÉTIS   Canadian aboriginal community primarily in the prairie west of mixed Caucasian-Native descent.

MULTICULTURALISM   government policy of encouraging and supporting the maintenance of diverse cultural identities and practices within the framework of a liberal democratic pluralist society.

MULTINATIONAL COUNTRY   a country whose population comprises cultural communities sufficiently distinct to see themselves as separate nations.

MUNICIPALITIES   lowest tier of government in a federation, not enjoying constitutional status on a par with the national government or the constituent units.

NATION OF WILL   national community formed on basis of deliberate intent rather than reflective of some underlying ethnic or cultural identity.

NATIONAL COUNCIL   first or lower chamber of the Swiss parliament.

NATIVE AMERICANS   term for original inhabitants in the UNITED STATES; see ABORIGINAL PEOPLES.

NORTHERN TERRITORY   one of two self-governing Territories in the Commonwealth of Australia, operating under powers delegated by the federal parliament.

OBLASTI   one category comprising 46 of the 83 constituent units of the Russian federation enjoying less constitutional autonomy thant REPUBLICS; translates as 'provinces'.

POPULAR INITIATIVE   procedure of direct democracy whereby a determined number of citizens can instigate a referendum on a law or issue.

PROVINCES   official name of the constituent units in Canada, Argentina and South Africa.

REFERENDUM   procedure for popular consultation required for constitutional alteration in Australia and widely used in Swiss system for constitutional, sub-constitutional and other matters e.g. expenditures.

REGIONS   the three territorial divisions of the Belgian federation (Flanders, Wallonia, Brussels).

REPUBLICS   one category comprising 21 of the 83 constituent units of the Russian federation enjoying right to their own national language (unlike OBLASTI).

REVENUE-SHARING   arrangements or requirements for revenue from specified tax bases to be shared between orders of government according to an established formula.

ROYAL COMMISSION   formal executive inquiry in Canadian or Australian political system exercising considerable powers and enjoying full autonomy within their terms of reference.

SCHEDULED CASTES   constitutionally recognised lower CASTES.

STATES   name for the constituent units in the federations of Australia (6 States), Brazil (26 States), India (28 States), Mexico (31 States), Nigeria (36 States), United States of America (50 States).

SUPREME COURT   final court of appeal at apex of judicial system in such federal systems as the United States, Canada and Australia, covering constitutional as well as other public and private law matters.

TERRITORIAL MINORITIES   distinct social groups located or concentrated in particular geographic areas within a country rather than spread throughout the population.

UNION   term for the central government in India.

VERTICAL FISCAL TRANSFERS   intergovernmental grants between levels of government to compensate for FISCAL IMBALANCE.

WHITE AUSTRALIA POLICY   legislation passed soon after Federation in Australia to restrict immigration of non-European peoples and abandoned in the 1960s and 1970s.

Contributors

NICHOLAS ARONEY, Reader in Law, TC Beirne School of Law, University of Queensland, Australia

BALVEER ARORA, Professor, Political Science, Centre for Political Studies, Jawaharlal Nehru University, India

PETRA BENDEL, Associate Professor, Central Institute for Regional and Area Studies, Friedrich-Alexander-University Erlangen-Nuremberg, Germany

IRINA BUSYGINA, Professor, Department of Political Science, Moscow State Institute of International Relations and Director, Centre for Regional Political Studies, Moscow State Institute of International Relations (MGIMO), Russia

CÉSAR COLINO, Associate Professor, Universidad Nacional de Educación a Distancia, Spain

FRANK DELMARTINO, Emeritus Professor, Katholieke Universiteit Leuven and former director, Institute for International and European Policy, Belgium

HUGUES DUMONT, Professor, Constitutional Law and European Law, Law Faculty, Facultés Universitaires Saint-Louis, Belgium

MARCUS FARO DE CASTRO, Dean, Faculty of Law, Brasília University, Brazil

ASSEFA FISEHA, Associate Professor and Director, Institute of Federalism and Legal Studies, Ethiopian Civil Service College, Ethiopiastria

THOMAS FLEINER, Director, Institute of Federalism, University of Fribourg, Switzerland

ALAIN-G. GAGNON, FRSC, Canada Research Chair in Quebec and Canadian Studies, Université du Québec à Montréal, Department of Political Science, Canada

MOHAMMED HABIB, Assistant Professor of Law, Addis Ababa University, Ethiopia

ANDREAS HEINEMANN-GRÜDER, Senior Researcher, Bonn International Centre for Conversion and Associate Professor, University of Bonn, Germany

MAYA HERTIG RANDALL, Professor, Faculty of Law, University of Geneva, Switzerland

JOHN KINCAID, Professor, Government and Public Service and Director, Robert B. and Helen S. Meyner Center for the Study of State and Local Government, Lafayette College, USA

GILBERTO MARCOS ANTONIO RODRIGUES, Professor, Faculty of Law, Universidade Católica de Santos, Brazil

LUIS MORENO, Research Professor, Centre for Human and Social Sciences, Spanish National Research Council (CSIC), Spain

RICHARD SIMEON, Professor, Political Science and Law, University of Toronto, Canada

ROLAND STURM, Professor, Institut for Political Science, Friedrich-Alexander-University Erlangen-Nuremberg, Germany

ROTIMI T. SUBERU, Professor, Political Science and International Relations, Bennington College, USA

SÉBASTIEN VAN DROOGHENBROECK, Professor, Human Rights Law and Constitutional Law, Law Faculty, Facultés Universitaires Saint-Louis, Belgium

Participating Experts

We gratefully acknowledge the input of the following experts who participated in the theme of Diversity and Unity in Federal Countries. While participants contributed their knowledge and experience, they are in no way responsible for the contents of this booklet.

Habtamu Abino, House of Federation, Ethiopia
Adigun Agbaje, University of Ibadan, Nigeria
Jeleel Agboola, All Nigerian Peoples Party (ANPP), Nigeria
Remi Aiyede, University of Ibadan, Nigeria
Sonia Akinbiyi, Ogun State Judiciary, Nigeria
Svetlana Akkieva, KBIGI Nalchik Kabardino-Balkarskiy nauchnyj Tsentr, Russia
James Allan, University of Queensland, Australia
Enrique Álvarez Conde, Universidad Rey Juan Carlos, Spain
Simone Alves da Silva, Universidade de Brasília, Brazil
George Anderson, Forum of Federations, Canada
Guillermo Arbelaez, Association de Papaya, Switzerland
Xavier Arbós i Marín, Universitat de Girona, Spain
Victor Armony, Université du Québec à Montréal, Canada
Nicholas Aroney, University of Queensland, Australia
Balveer Arora, Jawaharlal Nehru University, India
Joseba Arregi Aranburu, Universidad de País Vasco, Spain
Getachew Assefa, Addis Ababa University, Ethiopia
John Ayoade, University of Ibadan, Nigeria
Ewnetu B.Debela, Minstry of Federal Affairs, Ethiopia
Earl M. Baker, Earl Baker Consulting, USA
Lidija Basta Fleiner, International Research and Consulting Centre, Switzerland
Christian Behrendt, Université de Liège, Belgium
I. B. Bello-Imam, Lead City University, Nigeria
Petra Bendel, Central Institute for Area Studies, Germany

Solomon Benjamin, Nigerian Institute of Social and Economic Research
(NISER), Nigeria
Ann Bennison, Brisbane City Council, Australia
Katharine Betts, Swinburne University, Australia
Million Beyene, Walta Information Center, Ethiopia
Rumkini Bhaya Nair, Indian Institute of Technology, India
Vijay Bhushan, Former Secretary to the Government of India, India
Jim Bickerton, St. Francis Xavier University, Canada
Nicolas Bonbled, Université Catholique de Louvain, Belgium
Núria Bosch Roca, Universitat de Barcelona, Spain
Rogério Boueri, Instituto de Pesquisa Econômica Aplicada, Brazil
Alan Box Jangala, Central Land Council, Australia
Eva Brems, Universiteit Gent, Belgium
A.J. Brown, Griffith Law School, Australia
Irina Busygina, Moscow State Institute of International Relations (MGIMO),
Russia
Benjamin Cadranel, Gouvernement de la Région de Bruxelles-Capitale, Belgium
Urs Cadruvi, Lia Rumantscha, Switzerland
Miquel Caminal Badia, Universitat de Barcelona, Spain
Vicente Carlos Y Plá Trevas, Ministério da Justiça, Brazil
Vinicius Carvalho, Secretaria Especial de Direitos Humanos, Brazil
Matteo Casoni, Osservatorio linguistico della Svizzera italiana, Switzerland
Ariel Cecilio Garces Pares, Núcleo de Assuntos Estratégicos, Brazil
Gustavo Cesário, Confederaçã Nacional de Municípios, Brazil
Rupak Chattopadhyay, Forum of Federations, Canada
Rekha Chowdhary, University of Jammu, India
Vicente Cidade, Secretaria de Integração Regional, Estado do Parà, Brazil
Richard L. Cole, University of Texas at Arlington, USA
Kumlachew Dagne, InterAfrica Group, Ethiopia
Gianni d'Amato, Swiss Forum for Migration and Population Studies,
Switzerland
Nathaniel Danjibo, Nigerian Institute of Social and Economic Research
(NISER), Nigeria
Roque de Barros Laraia, Universidade Católica de Santos, Brazil
Rui de Britto Alvares Affonso, Instituto de Economia – UNICAMP, Brazil
Pierre-Olivier De Broux, Facultés Universitaires Sainte-Louis, Belgium
Xavier Delgrange, Facultés Universitaires Sainte-Louis, Belgium
Frank Delmartino, Katholieke Universiteit Leuven, Belgium
Daniel Demissie, House of Federation, Ethiopia
Isabelle Dirkx, Comité des Régions, Belgium
Christos Doulkeridis, Parlement Francophone Bruxellois, Belgium
Hugues Dumont, Facultés Universitaires Sainte-Louis, Belgium
Howard Duncan, Metropolis Project, Canada
Festus Egwaikhide, University of Ibadan, Nigeria

Rosani Evangelista da Cunha, Ministério do Desenvolvimento Social, Brazil
Marcus Faro de Castro, Universidade de Brasília, Brazil
Adugna Feyissa, Ethiopian Press Agency, Ethiopia
Mikhail Filippov, Binghamton University, Russia
Assefa Fiseha, Institute of Federalism and Legal Studies, Ethiopia
Thomas Fleiner, Institute of Federalism, Switzerland
Marie-Claire Foblets, Katholieke Universiteit Leuven, Belgium
Robert Freeman, Pennsylvania House of Representatives, USA
IIdar Gabdrafikov, CER UMCRAN, Russia
Alain-G. Gagnon, Université du Québec à Montréal, Canada
Laurence Gallez, Parlement Bruxellois, Belgium
Maria Jesús García Morales, Universitat Autònoma de Barcelona, Spain
Addisu Gebreigzabhier, Ministry of Federal Affairs, Ethiopia
Dirk Gerdes, University of Heidelberg, Germany
Dagnchew Gione, Ethiopian Television (ETV), Ethiopia
Kristin Good, Dalhousie University, Canada
Mireia Grau i Creus, Institut d'Estudis Autonòmics, Spain
Mikhail Grigorevich Mironyuk, Moscow State Institute of International Relations (MGIMO), Russia
Denis Grimberghs, Centre Démocrate Humaniste, Belgium
Fátima Guerreiro, Fórum Fiscal dos Estados, Brazil
Mohammed Habib, Addis Ababa University, Ethiopia
David Haljan, Katholieke Universiteit Leuven, Belgium
Gerda Hauck, House of Religions - Dialogue of Cultures, Switzerland
Werner Hauck, Language Services - Swiss Federal Chancellery, Switzerland
Sonja Haug, Federal Office for Migration and Refugees, Germany
Andreas Heinemann-Grüder, Bonn International Center for Conversion (BICC), Russia
Rodney Hero, University of Notre Dame, USA
Maya Hertig Randall, University of Geneva, Switzerland
Gerhard Hirscher, Hanns-Seidel-Foundation, Germany
Josh Hjartarson, Ontario Ministry of Intergovernmental Affairs, Canada
Grant Holly, Université de Montréal, Canada
Christine Horevoets, Cour constitutionnelle, Belgium
Babagana Ibrahim, Federal Road Safety Corps, Nigeria
Ade Isumonah, University of Ibadan, Nigeria
Billy Jampijinpa Bunter, Central Land Council, Australia
Martin Japanangka Johnson, Lajamanu Community Government Council, Australia
Sofiri Joab-Peterside, Center for Advanced Social Science, Nigeria
Gary Johns, ACIL Tasman, Australia
Kimberley Johnson, Barnard College, USA
Kailash K. K., Panjab University, India
Oleg Kashirskiy, Higher School of Economics, Russia

John Kincaid, Meyner Center, USA
KiDane Kiros Bitsue, Addis Ababa University, Ethiopia
Junichiro Koji, University of Ottawa, Canada
Diana Kolmogorova, Perm Regional Administration, Russia
Michael Krennerich, University of Erlangen Nuremberg, Germany
Cristina Kruck, Rroma Foundation, Switzerland
Meltem Kulacatan, University of Erlangen Nuremberg, Germany
Gopa Kumar, University of Kerala, India
Ashutosh Kumar, Panjab University, India
Deepak Kumar Singh, Panjab University, India
Alexander Vladimirovich Kynev, Foundation of Information Policy
Development, Russia
Kiera L. Ladner, University of Manitoba, Canada
Stephen Lafenwa, University of Ibadan, Nigeria
Vinay Lal, University of California, Los Angeles, India
Karl-Heinz Lambertz, Deutschsprachige Gemeinschaft Belgiën, Belgium
Simone Lavelle Godoy de Oliveira, Universidade Católica de Santos, Brazil
J. Wesley Leckrone, Widener University, USA
Ana Célia Lobo Silva, Universidade Católica de Santos, Brazil
Mark Lopez, Competitive Advantage, Australia
Alberto López Basaguren, Universidad de País Vasco, Spain
Deb Lovely, Griffith University, Australia
André Luiz de Figueiredo Lázaro, Ministério da Educação, Brazil
Clem Macintyre, University of Adelaide, Australia
Malcolm MacLaren, National Centre of Competence in Research: Challenges
to Democracy, Switzerland
Fred Maia, Ministério da Cultura, Brazil
Joseph Marbach, Seton Hall University, USA
Gilberto Marcos Antônio Rodrigues, Universidade Católica de Santos, Brazil
John Markakis, Ministry of Federal Affairs, Ethiopia
Luc Martens, Flemish Parliament, Belgium
Kevin Martin, Queensland University of Technology, Australia
Enric Martínez Herrera, Centro de Estudios Políticos y Constitucionales, Spain
John McCartney, Lafayette College, USA
Marcio Meira, Fundação Nacional do Índio, Brazil
Marcio Meirelles, Secretaria de Cultura da Bahia, Brazil
Fernanda Menezes, Banco do Brasil, Brazil
Oleg Michailovich Tsvetkov, UNC RAN, Russia
Julio Miragaya, Ministério da Integração Nacional, Brazil
Wim Moesen, Katholieke Universiteit Leuven, Belgium
Pampa Mukherjee, Panjab University, India
Markus Müller, Ministry of Economic Affairs - Baden, Germany
Solomon Negus, Ethiopian Civil Service College, Ethiopia
Leonhard Neycken, Ministerium der Deutschsprachige Gemeinschaft, Belgium

Valdimir Nikolaevich Streletsky, Moscow State University, Russia
Tiplut Nongbri, Jawaharlal Nehru Univeristy, India
Xose Manuel Núñez Seixas, Universidade de Santiago, Spain
Alaba Ogunsanwo, Lead City University, Nigeria
Stanley Okafor, University of Ibadan, Nigeria
Wale Okediran, Primero Consultancy Limited, Nigeria
Eyene Okpanachi, Kebbi State Ministry of Education, Nigeria
Bayo Okunade, University of Ibadan, Nigeria
Abubakar Oladeji, Nigerian Institute of Social and Economic Research
(NISER), Nigeria
Ayo Olukotun, Lead City University, Nigeria
Shola Omotola, Redeemer's University, Nigeria
Muhammad Oppliger, Ahmadiyya Muslim Jamaat, Switzerland
Oyeleye Oyediran, Center for Policy Research Trust, Nigeria
Surendra Pachauri, Indian Administrative Service, India
Martin Papillon, University of Ottawa, Canada
Maria Paula Dallari Bucci, Ministério da Educação, Brazil
Heinrich Pehle, University of Erlangen Nuremberg, Germany
Manuel Pérez Yruela, Consejo Superior de Investigaciones Científicas, Spain
Bill Pincus, University of Queensland, Australia
Constantin Pitsch, Federal Agency for Culture, Switzerland
Giovanni Poggeschi, Universita degli Studi di Lecce, Russia
Irene Pogoson, University of Ibadan, Nigeria
Anna Pomian, Hanns-Seidel-Foundation, Germany
Scott Prasser, University of the Sunshine Coast, Australia
Mahendra Pratap Singh, University of Delhi, India
Joachim Ragnitz, Ifo Institute for Economic Research, Germany
Suri Ratnapala, University of Queensland, Australia
Paula Losada, Subchefia de Assuntos Federativos, Brazil
Steffi Redmann, Federal Office for Migration and Refugees, Germany
Tsegaye Regassa, Ethiopian Civil Service College, Ethiopia
Cleuza Repulho, United Nations Educational, Scientific and Cultural
Organization (UNESCO), Brazil
Ferran Requejo Coll, Universitat Pompeu Fabra, Spain
Philip Resnick, University of British Columbia, Canada
Fernando Rezende, Fundação Getulio Vargas, Brazil
Sérgio Ricardo Miranda Nazaré, Banco do Brasil, Brazil
Aurélio Rios, Procuradoria-Geral da República, Brazil
Paulo Roberto Ziulkoski, Confederação Nacional de Municípios, Brazil
Joan Romero González, Universitat de València, Spain
Peter Ronad dSouza, Indian Institute of Advanced Studies, India
Edson Santos, Presidência da República, Brazil
Asha Sarangi, Jawaharlal Nehru University, India
Cheryl Saunders, University of Melbourne, Australia

Rekha Saxena, Centre For Federal Studies, India
Hans-Christoph Schmitt, University of Erlangen Nuremberg, Germany
Leslie Seidle, Institute for Research on Public Policy, Canada
Esther Seijas Villadangos, Universidad de León, Spain
Sandeep Shastri, International Academy for Creative Teaching, India
Nasseema Siddiqui, Circle of Canadians, Canada
Alexey Sidorenko, Carnegie Moscow, Russia
Maria Silva, Presidência da República, Brazil
Antonia Simbine, Nigerian Institute of Social and Economic Research
(NISER), Nigeria
Richard Simeon, University of Toronto, Canada
Dave Sinardet, Universiteit Antwerpen, Belgium
Bhupinder Singh Brar, Panjab University, India
Amarjit Singh Narang, Indira Gandhi National Open University, India
Juan José Solozábal, Universidad Autónoma de Madrid, Spain
Janaki Srinivasan, Panjab University, India
Roland Sturm, University of Erlangen Nuremberg, Germany
Rotimi Suberu, University of Ibadan, Nigeria
Kham Khan Suan, Banaras Hindu University, India
Joan Subirats Humet, Universitat Autònoma de Barcelona, Spain
Alan Tarr, Rutgers University-Camden, USA
Greg Taylor, Monash University, Australia
Marcos Terena, Comitê Intertribal (ITC), Brazil
Fikre Mariam Tesfaye, The Monitor, Ethiopia
Ivan Timofeev, Moscow State Institute of International Relations (MGIMO),
Russia
Getachew Tsere, Ethiopian Television (ETV), Ethiopia
Luc Turgeon, University of Toronto, Canada
Anne Twomey, University of Sydney, Australia
Gebru Gebre MariamUttura, United Ethiopian Democratic Forces, Ethiopia
Maria Unrau, Friedrich Ebert Foundation, Russia
Milena Valerievna Gligich-Zolotareva, Council of Federation, Russia
Astrid Van Der Haegen, Facultés Universitaires Sainte-Louis, Belgium
Sébastien Van Drooghenbroeck, Facultés Universitaires Sainte-Louis, Belgium
Dirk Vanheule, Universiteit Antwerpen, Belgium
Sarah Vaughan, Addis Ababa University, Ethiopia
Jan Velaers, Universiteit Antwerpen, Belgium
Magali Verdonck, Facultés Universitaires Sainte-Louis, Belgium
Leonid Viktorovich Smirnyagin, Moscow State University, Russia
Carles Viver Pi-Sunyer, Institut d'Estudis Autonòmics, Spain
Gautam Vohra, Development Research & Action Group (DRAG), India
Siddiq Wahid, Islamic University of Science and Technology, India
Sara Walter, Lafayette College, USA
David Wilkins, University of Minnesota-Twin Cities, USA

John Williams, University of Adelaide, Australia
David Woglom, Lafayette College, USA
Hassan Bajwa Yahya, Ahmadiyya Muslim Jamaat, Switzerland
Kassa G. Yohanes, Forum for Federalism and Democracy, Ethiopia
Semir Yusuf, Addis Ababa University, Ethiopia
Bilkisu Yusuf, Citizen Communications, Nigeria
Ricard Zapata-Barrero, Universitat Pompeu Fabra, Spain
Temesgen Zewdie, Parliament of Ethiopia, Ethiopia
Dr. Petra Zimmermannsteinhart, House of Federation, Ethiopia
Natalya Zubarevich, Moscow State University, Russia
Navjot, Panjab University, India

Diversity and Unity in Federal Countries
Edited by César Colino and Luis Moreno
Senior Editor, John Kincaid

Published for the Forum of Federations and the International Association of Centers
for Federal Studies (IACFS)
Global Dialogue on Federalism, Book Series, Volume 7

Examines the balance of diversity and unity in twelve federal or federal-type countries
(Australia, Belgium, Brazil, Canada, Ethiopia, Germany, India, Nigeria, Russian, Spain,
Switzerland and the United States of America). Leading scholars and practitioners
illustrate the current political, socio-economic, spatial, and cultural diversity in their
country before delving into the role that social, historical and political factors have
had in shaping the present balance of diversity and unity. Authors assess the value
that is placed on diversity by examining whether present institutional arrangements
and public policies either restrict or enhance it, and address the future challenges
of balancing diversity and unity in an increasingly populated and mobile world.

Authors include: Nicholas Aroney, Balveer Arora, Petra Bendel, Irina Busygina, César
Colino, Frank Delmartino, Hugues Dumont, Marcus Faro de Castro, Assefa Fiseha,
Thomas Fleiner, Alain-G. Gagnon, Mohammed Habib, Andreas Heinemann-Grüder,
Maya Hertig Randall, John Kincaid, Gilberto Marcos Antonio Rodrigues, Luis Moreno,
Richard Simeon, Roland Sturm, Rotimi T. Suberu, Sébastien Van Drooghenbroeck.

JOHN KINCAID is Professor of Government and Public Service and director of the
Robert B. and Helen S. Meyner Center for the Study of State and Local Government
at Lafayette College, Easton, Pennsylvania.
LUIS MORENO is a Research Professor at the Centre for Human and Social Sciences,
Spanish National Research Council (CSIC), Spain.
CÉSAR COLINO is an Associate Professor at the Universidad Nacional de Educación a
Distancia, Spain.

December 2008
6 x 9 12 maps

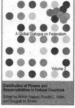

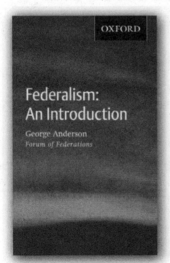

Federations: What's new in federalism worldwide

Edited by Rod Macdonell
Published three times per year

- A specialized magazine, geared toward practitioners of federalism, with stories on current events in federal countries and how these relate to their federal systems of government
- Theme-related articles that explore specific aspects of federal governance worldwide
- Each issue offers a snapshot of federalism in its current state around the world

I really enjoy reading the magazine. When I have finished reading an edition I have the sure sense that I am aware of the important events that are happening in most of the world's federations.

Arnold Koller, former
President of Switzerland

Send orders to

ORDER FORM: Fax to +1 (613) 244-3372

Please bill me (check one):

- ☐ $25 CDN per year in Canada
- ☐ €20 in euro zone
- ☐ $25 U.S. elsewhere

By: ☐ VISA ☐ Mastercard

Credit Card number:_____

Expiry: _____/ _____/ _____

Signature: _____

Telephone/email: _____

Ship books to:_____

Name:_____

Organization:_____

Street:_____

City:_____

Prov./State:_____ Postal/Zip code:_____

Forum Publications / www.forumfed.org/en/products

Please send me

☐ Forumfed – electronic newsletter and email updates.	No charge
☐ Handbook of Federal Countries 2005	CA $65.00
☐ Dialogues on Constitutional Origins, Structure, and Change in Federal Countries.	CA $13.00
☐ Dialogues on Distribution of Powers and Responsibilities in Federal Countries.	CA $13.00
☐ Dialogues on Legislative, Executive, and Judicial Governance in Federal Countries.	CA $13.00
☐ Dialogues on the Practice of Fiscal Federalism: Comparative Perspectives.	CA $13.00
☐ Dialogues on Foreign Relations in Federal Countries.	CA $13.00
☐ Dialogues on Local Government and Metropolitan Regions in Federal Countries.	CA $13.00
☐ Foreign Relations in Federal Countries.	CA $35.00
☐ Video: The Challenge of Diversity. /personal use for classroom	CA $20.00
for educational broadcast.	CA $60.00
☐ Federalism in a Changing World.	CA $65.00
☐ The Art of Negotiation.	CA $25.00

Total: _____

Postage

North America: $5.00 CAD first book, $1.50 each additional.
Overseas: $5.50 CAD first book, $2.00 each additional)

Subtotal: _____

California/N.Y. State residents please add 8.25% sales tax: _____

Canadian residents please add 6% GST (GST number R132094343): _____

Total: _____

Payment

☐ Payment or credit card information must accompany order.

Cheque/money order (Made payable to McGill-Queen's University Press).

☐ VISA ☐ MasterCard

Credit Card number:_____

Expiry: _____/ _____/ _____

Signature: _____

Telephone/email: _____

Ship books to:_____

Name:_____

Street:_____

City:_____

Prov./State:_____ Postal/Zip code:_____

Forum of Federations
THE GLOBAL NETWORK ON FEDERALISM

700-325 Dalhousie,
Ottawa ON K1N 7G2 Canada

Tel.: 613.244.3360
Fax.: 613.244.3372

Notes

Notes

Notes

Notes

INTERGOVERNMENTAL RELATIONS
IN FEDERAL SYSTEMS

A Global Dialogue on Federalism publications available

BOOK SERIES
Constitutional Origins, Structure, and Change in Federal Countries (2005), Volume 1
Distribution of Powers and Responsibilities in Federal Countries (2006), Volume 2
Legislative, Executive, and Judicial Governance in Federal Countries (2006), Volume 3
The Practice of Fiscal Federalism: Comparative Perspectives (2007), Volume 4
Foreign Relations in Federal Countries (2009), Volume 5
Local Government and Metropolitan Regions in Federal Systems (2009), Volume 6

BOOKLET SERIES
Dialogues on Constitutional Origins, Structure, and Change in Federal Countries (2005), Volume 1
Dialogues on Distribution of Powers and Responsibilities in Federal Countries (2005), Volume 2
Dialogues on Legislative, Executive, and Judicial Governance in Federal Countries (2006), Volume 3
Dialogues on the Practice of Fiscal Federalism: Comparative Perspectives (2006), Volume 4
Dialogues on Foreign Relations in Federal Countries (2007), Volume 5
Dialogues on Local Government and Metropolitan Regions in Federal Countries (2007), Volume 6
Dialogues on Diversity and Unity in Federal Countries (2008), Volume 7

Select Global Dialogue publications are available in other languages including
Arabic, French, German, Portuguese and Spanish. For more information on
what is available, visit www.forumfed.org.

A Global Dialogue on Federalism
Booklet Series
Volume 8

INTERGOVERNMENTAL RELATIONS
IN FEDERAL SYSTEMS

EDITED BY RUPAK CHATTOPADHYAY
AND KARL NERENBERG

Published by

Forum of Federations

and

iacfs
INTERNATIONAL ASSOCIATION OF
CENTERS FOR FEDERAL STUDIES

Marketed by

McGill-Queen's University Press
Montreal & Kingston • London • Ithaca

This publication was produced with generous financial support from the Swiss
Agency for Development and Cooperation, the Government of Canada and
the Secrétariat aux affaires intergouvernementales canadiennes, Government
of Québec, Canada.

Library and Archives Canada Cataloguing in Publication

Dialogues on intergovernmental relations in federal systems / edited by Rupak
Chattopadhyay and Karl Nerenberg.

(Global dialogue on federalism ; v. 8)
Text in English and French.
ISBN 978-0-7735-3656-2

     1. Federal government. 2. Central-local government relations.
I. Chattopadhyay, Rupak II. Nerenberg, Karl
III. International Association of Centers for Federal Studies
IV. Forum of Federations V. Series: Global dialogue on federalism v. 8

JC355.D525 2010   321.02   C2009-907163-0

Printed and bound in Canada by Imprimerie Gauvin

Contents

Preface

We are pleased to introduce this booklet, Volume Eight in the Global Dialogue Booklet series, which is devoted to the topic of intergovernmental relations in thirteen federal or federal-type countries/regions. The featured countries/regions are: Argentina, Austria, Australia, Brazil, Canada, the European Union, Germany, India, Nigeria, South Africa, Spain, Switzerland and the United States. Each of these countries/regions has something unique to bring to this important examination of a topic for which there is not yet a common discourse and lexicon internationally.

Over-all, what a reader might conclude from this Booklet is that the subject of intergovernmental relations is an area where much study and investigation is still needed. The founding documents of most federations or federal-type countries/regions make virtually no reference to the rules, guidelines or norms governing cooperation and communication between and among governmental entities. Indeed, as this collection of articles shows, for almost all federal or federal-type systems, intergovernmental relations are still very much a work in progress. Much of what takes place in the intergovernmental domain, in all the countries/regions analyzed, is *ad hoc* and based on circumstance, culture and custom, rather than law and regulation.

It is impossible, of course, to imagine a system that entailed more than one order or level could function without some generally agreed means for cooperation and communication between and among the entities of government. Yet, this collection of articles underlines the fact that both those who practice and those who study federalism have only quite recently turned their attention to the matter of intergovernmental relations; and, as they have done so, they have developed very different ways of conceptualizing and describing the subject.

That is why booklets such as this one, and the series of which it is a part, can be of such value. They can provide practitioners and researchers alike with a window into the real-life challenges of federalism in vastly different political, cultural and economic circumstances. We hope that, in so doing, we help improve both the practice and the understanding of federalism as a world-wide phenomenon.

In due course this booklet will be followed by a more comprehensive book on the same topic, wherein the authors of the booklet explore the theme in further detail. Both publications, which are part of the Global Dialogue on Federalism Series, are the outcome of a greater project led by two partner organizations, the Forum of Federations and the International Association of Centers for Federal Studies.

The Global Dialogue program explores federal governance by theme and aims to bring experts together to inspire new ideas and fill a gap in the comparative literature on federal governance. After presenting the eighth booklet in five years, we note that these handy publications are becoming an indispensable reference document on their own, delivering instant comparative information on various topics in a concise format. It is not surprising that the previous volumes proved to be very popular and have been translated into numerous languages, including Arabic and Kurdish.

As much as these booklets have their own standing, they also continue to fulfill their original task related to the books. The number of books sold is steadily growing and will increase this coming year with the publication of Volume 7, *Diversity and Unity in Federal Countries.*

In this Booklet, the various aspects of the practice of intergovernmental relations are described in country chapters entitled "Dialogue Insights". The chapters are introduced by a text of comparative reflections written by Johanne Poirier and Cheryl Saunders. A glossary at the end of the booklet enhances the knowledge-sharing and educational vocation of this publication. It is expected that Volume Eight will be translated into Arabic, French, German and Spanish, following in the footsteps of previous volumes.

The overarching aim of each of these articles is to explain how the various orders of government in each federation or federal-type system relate to each other. Those "intergovernmental relations" include the relationship of the centre or federal government with the constituent units (states, cantons, provinces, etc.) as well as relations between and among constituent entities. There are cases where the "centre" and all the entities must deal with each other; other times where the entities cooperate as a group; and yet others where relations are bilateral or based on smaller sub-groupings. In fact, the articles in this booklet show that intergovernmental relations are characterized by a great variety of permutations and combinations.

Within this general framework arise important questions, such as:

☐ How does each country's unique history affect the way it carries out intergovernmental relations?

☐ How are social and regional inequalities addressed?

☐ What does the Constitution or fundamental law have to say about relations between and among orders of government?

□ What has been the history and evolution of intergovernmental relations, especially in relation to constitutional change and evolution?

□ Are there both formal and informal institutions of cooperation and coordination?

□ Where does one find "intertwined" roles and responsibilities and what mechanisms exist for accommodating them?

□ What is the financial/fiscal aspect of intergovernmental collaboration and cooperation, and how does it operate in the various cases?

□ What is the importance of personal relations between and among key political actors in the various orders of government?

□ How are disputes and conflicts managed?

These are only a small number of the questions that this series of articles addresses. As with many federal systems, the approach of this Booklet is somewhat asymmetric. The articles do not all answer the same questions, in identical format. True to their own circumstances and cultures, the authors have taken a diverse approach to the subject, a diversity that underscores the richness and complexity of federalism as it is practiced in the real world. In fact, that vital and rich diversity is itself an outcome of the Global Dialogue process and methodology.

What makes this booklet and book series distinct and unique is the process by which the publications are generated. Each theme process entails multiple stages, starting with the selection of a "theme coordinator". It is this person's task to create an internationally comprehensive set of questions covering institutional provisions and how they work in practice, based on the most current research. These sets of questions are the foundation of the program, as they guide the dialogue at the roundtables and ensure consistency in the book chapters. The roundtables themselves are led by a "country coordinator", and are organized concurrently in twelve chosen countries.

To create the most accurate picture of the situation in each country, the country coordinators invite a group of practicing and academic experts with diverse viewpoints and experience who are prepared to share with and learn from others in a non-politicized environment. At the end of the day, the coordinators are equipped to write an article that reflects the highlights of the dialogue from each country roundtable. The articles presented here have been generated from such an exchange.

Once each country has held its roundtable, representatives gather at an international roundtable to identify commonalities and differences and to generate new insights. Such insights are incorporated into the country chapters in the aforementioned theme book. The chapters reflect the fact that their authors were able to explore the theme from a global vantage point, resulting in a truly comparative exploration of the topic.

The success of the Global Dialogue Program depends fully on the engagement of a variety of organizations and dedicated individuals. For

their generous financial support we would like to thank the Government
of Canada, the Government of Québec and the Swiss Agency for
Development and Cooperation. The International Roundtable in New Delhi
was made possible with generous support from the Inter-State Council
Secretariat of the Government of India and to V.N. Alok of the Indian
Institute of Public Administration for helping organize the international
roundtable. We also wish in particular to acknowledge the experts who
took part in the dialogue events for providing a diversity of perspectives
that helped to shape the articles themselves. Johanne Poirier and Cheryl
Saunders the Theme Coordinators, John Kincaid Senior Editor of the
book series, and the rest of the Global Dialogue Editorial Board have
offered their invaluable advice and expertise. Thank you to Alan Fenna for
doing the painstaking work of creating the glossary. We would like to
acknowledge the support offered by several staff members at the Forum of
Federations: Rhonda Dumas, Libby Johnston, Phillip Gonzalez, Roderick
Macdonell, Chris Randall, and Carl Stieren. We would like to thank the
staff at Imprimerie Gauvin for their important assistance in the printing
process. Finally, we thank the staff at McGill-Queen's University Press for
offering their support and advice throughout the publication process.

The Global Dialogue on Federalism Series continues the Forum of
Federations' tradition of publishing either independently or in partnership
with other organizations.

The Forum has produced a variety of books and multimedia material.
For further information on the Forum's publications and activities, refer
to the Forum's website at www.forumfed.org. The website contains links to
other organizations and an on-line library which includes Global Dialogue
articles and chapters.

The increasing body of literature produced by the Forum of Federations
and the International Association of Centers for Federal Studies aims to
encourage practitioners and scholars to use the knowledge gained to
devise new solutions and to join the many active participants around the
world in the growing international network on federalism. We welcome
feedback and suggestions on how these series can be improved to serve
this goal.

Rupak Chattopadhyay and Karl Nerenberg, Editors
Forum of Federations

INTERGOVERNMENTAL RELATIONS
IN FEDERAL SYSTEMS

Cooperative Mechanisms
and Intergovernmental Relations
in Federal Regimes

JOHANNE POIRIER / CHERYL SAUNDERS

Intergovernmental relations (IGR) are a feature of every federal regime. While federations differ in many respects, substantial interaction between orders of government is unavoidable and techniques for managing interdependence are varied and widespread. At the heart of the phenomenon are the many institutions and processes through which federal partners enter into relations with each other. These are the primary subject of this booklet

The Global Dialogue theme on Intergovernmental Relations is based around 13 case studies: twelve federations and the emerging quasi federal entity that is the EU. The case studies illustrate the wide variety of objectives pursued by central authorities, constitutive units (and increasingly municipalities) through IGR. These range from information sharing to policy coordination, from the elaboration of joint projects to coordinated law-making, from financial redistribution to the setting up of joint bodies and the establishment of mechanisms for dispute resolution. In Canada and Australia, IGR are even conceived by many as pragmatic substitutes for (unattainable) constitutional reforms.

IGR take different forms and shapes depending on country-specific historical, geographical, constitutional, structural, social, linguistic, religious and political factors. The design of IGR also differ within federations, according to the policy at stake and over time.

Some IGR are purely "horizontal", in the sense that they occur primarily between constituent units (CU). Others involve both the CU and federal authorities and are sometimes referred to as "vertical", although this term suggests a hierarchy between orders that does not formally exist in many federations. IGR are often multilateral (involving a number of federal partners, if not all). On the other hand, bilateral arrangements also are common: between neighbouring constitutive units to address trans-border

issues, for example, or between the center and a particular unit (particularly if the latter is culturally "distinct"). In this case, IGR can reflect and
foster asymmetrical arrangements in an asymmetrical federal society.

One question for this theme is whether, in the face of such diversity, a
comparative study of IGR is feasible? In fact, as this chapter shows, there
are considerable similarities, as well as notable differences between the
case studies used for this theme, both in terms of the main institutions and
processes for conducting IGR (A) and in terms of emerging trends and
common challenges (B).

A. Institutions and Processes of IGR

IGR: From Highly Institutionalised to Informal

The pattern of relations between federal partners range from legal
principles and institutions, embedded in Constitutions or legislation, to
a range of informal, largely opaque but essential connections across jurisdictional borders.

A number of factors influence preference for a more legalised form of
IGR. One is timing: in older federations, which typically developed from a
process of integration, relatively little thought was given to IGR at the time
the Constitution was adopted. In these federations, IGR developed gradually
as a response to political need (Canada, Australia, United States). By contrast, more recent federal regimes, many of which resulting from a process
of devolution or at the end of a dictatorial period, tend to favour more
structured, legalised or even constitutionalised forms of interaction
(Spain, South Africa, Brazil). Some systems hover between the two (India).

Another factor at play may be the legal tradition in which a federal system
is grounded. Hence, civil law federations are likely to be more legalistic
and seek to set out rules in formal text, than their more pragmatic
common law counterparts, for which many IGR require merely an exercise
of executive power. IGR are thus more institutionalised in Germany
than in Nigeria or Canada. Legal tradition also helps to explain why
Switzerland, an older federation formed by aggregation, has a range of
formal IGR mechanisms, while these are much rarer in the United States,
also an old federation formed in a broadly similar way. Similarly, while
the European Union has a mixed legal system, it is still largely influenced
by continental culture which tends to favour legalised forms of interaction.

Despite these differences of approach, two general propositions may be
made. First informal, personal relations between jurisdictions are important in all federations, either as a substitute for more formal arrangements
or as a complement to them. Secondly, in most federations it is possible
to detect a trend towards institutionalisation of IGR, although the USA
is a clear outlier. While formalisation has its draw-backs, it offers greater
certainty, enhances transparency and accountability and arguably suggests

greater respect for the balance between self-rule and joint rule. More formalised arrangements are also more likely to provide a base for judicial review. While in fact courts are rarely called upon to arbitrate IGR, the fact that they can do so, reinforces the rule of law in complex multi-level regimes.

Legislative institutions and techniques

A range of legislative techniques and institutions are associated with IGR. First, depending on their design, federal second chambers can provide a forum for the participation of constitutive units in federal policy making. The German Bundesrat is a case in point. Secondly, in some federations, of which the United States is an example, some agreements between constituent units require approval or ratification by the central legislature, giving the agreements themselves a degree of legal force.

Third, a range of legislative techniques facilitate coordination between the federation. Thus, in some federations, legislative or regulatory powers may be referred or delegated from one order to another order (Australia, Spain, Switzerland). In a technique of another kind, "mirror legislation" in which a model designed by one order is replicated by others ensure a degree of uniformity, despite a fragmentation of competences (Canada). Another technique lies in the enactment of a template – or "model" – law by one legislature, which can be replicated by others in exercise of their own power. EU "directives" which must be "transposed" through legislation in all of the 27 member states are a prime example of this technique which in theory combines both a degree of uniformity with responsiveness to local preferences. In practice, however, central rules may be so detailed as to curtail the legislative autonomy of CU (Spain).

In an example of a different kind, IGR in Switzerland are affected by direct democracy, since the people can exert a major influence on the modes of interaction between federal partners through the initiative and referendum. Even legally binding inter-cantonal treaties can be challenged through referenda. Direct democracy seems to facilitate relatively harmonious IGR, given the Swiss profound and historical commitment to cooperative relations, as well as respect for multiple identities and local differences.

Executive Mechanisms

Despite the significance of cooperative institutions and techniques involving the legislatures, IGR remain largely the prerogative of the executive branch, particularly in parliamentary systems.

The most significant institution for this purpose is the official forum in which Heads of the various orders of government meet in most federations (Argentina being an exception). Again, these may have arisen on a pragmatic basis (Canada), while others are provided for in legal text (Spain). The degree of formalisation does not appear to affect their importance or effectiveness however. Most conferences include the Head of the central government as well as those of CU. Increasingly, however, the Heads of the CU also meet to develop common strategies with regards to central authorities or to articulate their respective policies in areas of exclusive CU competences.

Such Conferences often attract media attention. Yet, most of the actual intergovernmental management flows from meetings between sectoral ministers, as well as between civil servants and policy advisors. The web of IG meetings and networks can be extremely dense.

Civil service

A non-politicised civil service seems to be key to effective IGR at the technical level. Professional civil servants can maintain effective relations, even in the face of open tensions at the political level. All case studies show that regardless of the degree of formalisation of IGR, personal relations, and informal interaction are essential elements of effective IGR.

Agreements between federal partners

Agreements are a significant method of coordination in all federations. In some cases, literally hundreds of such agreements are concluded each year (Canada, Spain). They are used to coordinate and harmonise action, to set up common institutions or outline cooperative procedures. They may include dispute resolution mechanisms. Some are vehicles for federal spending power: allowing for central influence on the exercise of the competences of constitutive units. In some cases, units are effectively forced to conclude agreements, in order to obtain funding which they often desperately need, arguably transforming this instrument of cooperative federalism into tools of coercion (for example, Austria, Canada, Australia, Spain, Switzerland).

While some agreements are clearly of a purely political nature, others are officially legally binding. In some cases, agreements are systematically published (Austria, Brazil, Spain, Switzerland), while in others, there is no formal mechanism for making them publicly available. (Australia, Canada).

Joint agencies and Independent Commissions

Another mechanism used in some federations to foster common action are joint agencies, with legal personality, and, in some cases, binding regulatory power (such as *consorcios* in Spain). In some federations, independent Commissions play a governance role in ways that affects multiple jurisdictions and which typically have an intergovernmental element (Australia, India, Nigeria).

II. Emerging Trends and Common Challenges

The thirteen case studies reveal that behind similarities and differences in terms of institutions and processes lie a number of underlying trends and challenges.

Emerging Horizontal Action

First, in recent years there appears to be a trend towards the development of horizontal relations. The Council of the Federation in Canada, the Council of the Australian Federation, the Conference of the *Länder* Governors in Austria or the Governors' Forum in Nigeria, illustrate this development. Whether institutionalised or not, horizontal relations seem to be primarily aimed at influencing national debates (and sometimes elaborating common strategies in the face of the centralising tendencies of federal authorities). In some federations, horizontal relations (re)create regional blocks (Nigeria, Canada, Brazil). At the technical level, however, they also seek to improve policy delivery with trans-border implications.

New Actors

Secondly, increasingly, policy making and implementation involve non-government actors, as well as political institutions which may, nor may not be formal "partners in the federation". These include First Nations, neighbouring countries and private actors, but perhaps, more generally, municipalities. This is so whether the local level is constitutionally recognised as a "third order" of government (South Africa, Brazil) or whether their importance flows from geography and demography (many metropolitan areas are larger and more populous than some CU. In some contexts, the local level plays such a central role, particularly in service delivery, that the traditional/conceptual "privileged" relationship between CU and the federal order is marginalised. Local authorities can even be caught in power politics between traditional federal actors (Brazil, Canada, South Africa).

The increasing importance of new actors complicates the traditional networks of vertical and horizontal IGR. Existing institutions and processes – largely designed to structure relations between two-orders of government – are rarely adapted to accommodate these new actors. There are some innovations, however, which deal with the integration of new participants in the IGR game. Hence, local governments have non-voting representation in the National Council of Provinces in South Africa. In Brazil, federal ministerial decrees in the area of health care are first negotiated in a tripartite arena composed of an equal number of federal, state and municipal orders. Ensuring participation of CU and local governments at the policy-elaboration stage seems to improve the effectiveness of policy implementation for which these orders are increasingly responsible.

IGR: tools of centralisation and constitutional (re)engineering?

The case studies suggest a general trend towards greater centralisation, despite some "administrative" devolution. IGR often allow the federal order to intervene more directly in CU affairs. In some instances, moreover, they implicitly transform CU into "agents" of the center, the latter providing major strategic directions, designs policies and provides funding. Such developments are particularly evident in Brazil and South Africa, but can also be observed in Australia, Canada and Spain.

The problem is not so great where the CU participate in the elaboration of these policies, as in the case of integrated federal systems. In Germany for instance, the CU can even veto central policy initiatives which negatively affect them. The phenomenon is more disturbing, however, when it effectively transforms dualist federations (in which each order in principle implements its own legislation and policies) into integrated ones, leaving the CU much less influential at the policy development phase.

In this sense, while IGR are essential to federal governance, they can affect the balance between self-rule (autonomy) and joint-rule (participation).

Efficiency and flexibility vs. accountability and the rule of law?

It is difficult to assess the actual impact of IGR on the effectiveness of public policy. Cooperation often is presented as a practical necessity, given the interconnected nature of competences and transborder issues. While coercion camouflaged as cooperation may limit policy innovation, it can also, in some cases contribute to better service delivery. While common standards may promote a form of equality, this may come at the cost of diversity, an integral value of federalism.

By contrast, a common concern that is raised in most of the thirteen case studies is the often opaque nature of IGR. Solutions negotiated between governments are presented to legislators as "faits accomplis", when they are presented at all. Even when parliamentarians can in theory exert some control over IGR (as in South Africa or Spain), they rarely do so. The case studies in this booklet suggest that, while IGR may be an unavoidable fact of federal life, and effective IGR may improve public services, they may also have a negative impact on citizen participation, transparency, political accountability and the rule of law.

Intergovernmental Relations in Argentina

WALTER F. CARNOTA, PH.D.

1. Terminology

There is an extensive Argentinean literature on intergovernmental relations although in Argentine political and legal circles writers do not often use the term, "intergovernmental relations". Over the years, a great many Argentine experts – betraying a legalistic approach – have preferred the expression "interjurisdictional relations". Others have opted to write about a particular type of cooperative federalism, *"federalismo de concertación"*, which they describe as an ideal, if unrealized, model for intergovernmental relations.

The term intergovernmental relations has only recently gained widespread currency in Argentina, as federal studies in the country have absorbed the influences of contemporary sociology, economics and political science.

2. Historical background

With the adoption, in 1853, of a national Constitution, Argentina became (technically, at any rate) a federal state. In doing so it reaffirmed previous pacts between the national government and the "historical" fourteen provinces (which did not include the most populous, Buenos Aires). In 1860, Buenos Aires rejoined the national family, after the constitution was modified to bring about a greater degree of decentralization.

During the period from 1816, when Argentina gained independence from

Spain, to the adoption of the 1853 Constitution, there were violent struggles between centralist and decentralizing political forces in the county. The fourteen provinces, excluding Buenos Aires, believed themselves to be subservient to the strong-willed rule of the Governor of the Province of Buenos Aires, Juan Manuel de Rosas, who was in power for two decades. Many of Rosas' opponents, who had gone into exile in Chile and Uruguay, helped draft the 1853 Constitution.

The first incarnation of Argentine federalism, that this constitution created, was rooted in the U.S. tradition of 1787. At the same time, the constitution drew on local sources, including the writings of Juan Bautista Alberdi, who championed a more centralized federal structure.

This type of federalism defined three main relationships between the national and the provincial spheres.

First, federal norms prevailed over provincial ones, according to a constitutional supremacy clause, which was patterned after that of the U.S. constitution.

Second, there is what we might call a "coordination axis", where delegated, concurrent and retained powers coexisted.

And third, provinces participated in the national Senate, as Senators formally represented the constituent units.

> Recurrent political and economic crises have triggered federal interventions in the governance of the provinces, which in turn tended to become more and more dependent on the federal government for financial support. Military governments exacerbated this tendency, since they gave themselves the power to remove provincial Governors and local officials whenever the spirit moved them.

Although this decentralized federalism existed in theory, until very recently Argentina lacked proper mechanisms to make its federalism effective. Recurrent political and economic crises have triggered federal interventions in the governance of the provinces, which in turn tended to become more and more dependent on the federal government for financial support. Military governments exacerbated this tendency, since they gave themselves the power to remove provincial Governors and local officials whenever the spirit moved them.

The constitutional reform of 1994 included significant clauses regarding federalism, mainly dealing with municipal and regional government and fiscal revenue-sharing. During the 1990s, the Menem Administration pursued a decentralized agenda in the fields of education and health services. This process was so thorough that by 2000 only one out of 121 public hospitals remained in federal hands.

3. Some numbers

Argentina has a population of nearly 40 million. It includes 23 provinces and the city of Buenos Aires, a federal district, which, since the most recent constitutional reform of 1994, has enjoying a considerable degree of autonomy. The Province of Buenos Aires is the country's largest and most populous.

Almost 45% of the country's population lives either in the Province or the city of Buenos Aires. In many ways, this fact alone accounts for a significant measure of asymmetry in Argentine federalism. Buenos Aires unavoidably exerts enormous political and economic influence over the rest of Argentina.

4. The main issues

Recent fiscal problems have made provincial governors particularly dependent on financial support from the federal government. Historically, there has been no adequate revenue-sharing scheme, although the 1994 constitutional reform mandated clearer criteria governing revenue sharing than had previously existed.

The national political parties (primarily, the Justicialista and the Radical parties) tend to act as "informal channels" for governors and other provincial and local leaders. This informal process means that key fiscal decisions are mainly concentrated in the city of Buenos Aires, which makes it very hard for an effective, balanced federalism to function. "Hyper-presidentialism", so prevalent in Latin America during the '90s, is still not remotely dead in Argentina.

Intergovernmental relations have thus evolved informally and, as it were, "in the shadows", lacking the necessary transparency and formal or informal settings for effective negotiations between and among orders of government. Some formal meetings between national and provincial ministers take place, for instance in the area of health. However, there are no permanent structures to implement the results of these meetings, with the result being that the relationship between the national and provincial governments is marked by discontinuity and lack of coordination.

Senators are empowered by the nation's Constitution to act as provincial representatives (all of the provinces and the city of Buenos Aires are allowed three Senators each). However, as in many other federal countries, Senators tend to represent their political parties over provincial interests

5. "Judicialization" of the federal agenda

Since Congress became less and less effective in dealing with people's very real grievances after the economic and financial crisis of 2001-2002, many sought remedies in the courts. For instance, as severe restrictions were placed on withdrawal of bank deposits (*"corralito financiero"*), customers began suing both banks and the national government. Federal judges faced an enormous workload in order to sort out these claims. Pensioners also massively sued the national government, as their pensions had also become a federal responsibility.

In this we can detect a larger trend: since the President and Congress seem unable to cope with many pressing problems on their own, political and economic matters, including those related to the practice of federal governance, tend to end up in court. The Supreme Court was largely overhauled during the Kirchner Administration of 2003 to 2007. Since 2003 the Supreme Court has handed down several key decisions. In the environmental field, for example, its decisions sought to achieve a balance among the national, provincial and municipal functions.

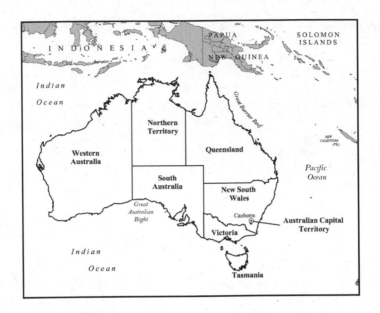

Intergovernmental Relations
in Australia: Increasing Engagement

JOHN PHILLIMORE

Australian federalism was not designed with intergovernmental relations uppermost in mind. Despite this, Australia has developed a comprehensive set of intergovernmental institutions and policy communities, and fostering cooperative relations between orders of government is high on the political agenda.

The expectation at "federation" in 1901 was that the two levels of government – the Commonwealth (the national or federal government of Australia) and the six State governments – could operate largely independent of each other. Following the US model, Australia's Constitution assigned to the Commonwealth government a limited number of (mostly concurrent) responsibilities, with the residual power being left to the States. Each level of government possesses a relatively complete set of legislative, judicial and executive institutions, based on British responsible government and the common law.

Two intergovernmental elements in the Constitution never operated as intended. The upper house of parliament, the Senate (comprising equal numbers of Senators from each State), rapidly became a party-based institution; while the Inter-State Commission had only two brief and undistinguished periods of existence.

Intergovernmental relations in Australia have been crafted pragmatically, taking into account changing conditions in Australian federalism more broadly. In the current context that means that there are increasingly shared functions, as government's role has widened and demands for national action in a globalized world have increased. There has also been an inexorable centralizing trend, as central government powers have increased through a combination of (relatively rare) constitutional amendments, expansive High Court decisions and a high degree of vertical fiscal imbalance.

As a result, intergovernmental engagement has been primarily led by the Commonwealth government, through a mixture of coercion, opportunism and cooperation. The Commonwealth has used a range of legal, institutional and political mechanisms. Emphasis has been on executive action, with only a limited role for legislatures, to pass necessary legislation. However, as part of community demands for improved governance processes and policy outcomes, there have been increasingly frequent calls (especially from business) to reduce waste and duplication and increase cross-border harmonization within the federation. And so, intergovernmental cooperation is firmly on the national agenda.

The Constitution provides for legal measures to facilitate intergovernmental cooperation. States and Territories can refer specific powers to the Commonwealth (e.g. for regulating corporations), and the Commonwealth can vest its jurisdiction in State courts where this is administratively convenient. Referral of powers is generally viewed suspiciously by States and used relatively rarely. However, governments frequently use mirror or model legislation to enable increased harmonization, while allowing some State variations. Uniform legislation – where one jurisdiction enacts legislation which others then adopt – is also used, and normally arises from intergovernmental discussions.

In recent years the most significant development in intergovernmental relations has been the establishment (in 1992) of the Council of Australian Governments (COAG). This is the peak intergovernmental council on which sit all first ministers and the Australian Local Government Association president.

While meetings of first ministers were not new, the COAG has taken intergovernmental relations to a new level of depth and sophistication. Although not formalized in an intergovernmental agreement, the Council meets regularly and sets much of the policy agenda for Ministerial Councils, and for governments more generally.

However, while the Council of Australian Governments might be thought of as the 'Cabinet' of the federation, it is clearly one where the Commonwealth government is first among equals. The Council is, in fact, an administrative entity of the Commonwealth: the Prime Minister calls the meetings, sets the agendas and prioritizes policy issues, reflecting the financial and policy power of the Commonwealth. An increasingly dense network of intergovernmental working parties and meetings of officials surrounds COAG, all of which are either attended or supported by secretariats within first ministers' departments.

> However, while the Council of Australian Governments might be thought of as the 'Cabinet' of the federation, it is clearly one where the Commonwealth government is first among equals. The Council is, in fact, an administrative entity of the Commonwealth: the Prime Minister calls the meetings, sets the agendas and prioritizes policy issues, reflecting the financial and policy power of the Commonwealth.

The other core intergovernmental bodies are Ministerial Councils. There are over 40 such Councils, dealing with a wide variety of specific policy areas, and involving responsible ministers from all jurisdictions (and sometimes New Zealand).

Councils meet at least annually to develop policy reform measures and take joint action. Most practice consensus decision-making, although some have special voting arrangements associated with particularly significant issues or with resource allocation. Increasingly, their agendas are linked to that of the Council of Australian Governments.

Outcomes from Ministerial Councils and major funding programs may be expressed in legislation, but are also now frequently codified in Intergovernmental Agreements. There are agreements of this sort on issues such as financial relations, food regulations, gene technology, water, and security issues.

Australia also has a long tradition of establishing independent regulatory, policy or advisory institutions to oversee important areas of public policy, such as fiscal equalization, food safety, water, energy and transport regu-lation, competition policy and vocational training. This is often achieved through a Ministerial Council and an Intergovernmental Agreement. Membership of these institutions is usually jointly selected by the Commonwealth and States to ensure they are not dominated by one or other level of government.

In 2006, following the Canadian example, the Council for the Australian Federation (consisting of State Premiers and Territory Chief Ministers) was established. Aimed at both achieving greater harmonization and influencing national debates, it remains to be seen how it will fare, especially in view of the Council of Australian Governments' increasing importance.

The election in 2007 of the Rudd Federal Labor Government has seen a much expanded role for the COAG, with more frequent meetings and the conclusion of a new Intergovernmental Agreement on federal financial relations, providing more flexibility (and funding) to the States.

The Rudd government has embarked upon a 'national reform agenda', extending the competition reforms of the 1990s with a new focus on human capital. A new independent Council of Australian Governments' Reform Council (with members nominated by the Commonwealth and the States) advises the COAG on a new outcomes-based financial reward system for policy reforms.

While it is as yet uncertain whether the new reform agenda will deliver the policy outcomes sought, it seems clear that intergovernmental relations in Australia will consist of an increasingly dense set of institutions and personal interactions, reflecting and accentuating the centralization of policy, management and administration within and between governments.

A key issue will be whether, and to what extent, the Council of Australian Governments, and intergovernmental relations more generally, will come up against particular limits. Those limits could be constitutional, organizational (there are already complaints of 'death by meetings'), political (can the new cooperative Council of Australian Governments survive potential changes of government?), or financial (will States continue to cooperate while remaining financially mendicant?). Overcoming these limits will be a major challenge for Australian intergovernmental relations in the future.

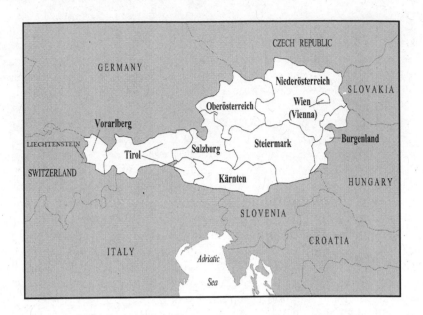

Cooperation and Coordination in Austrian Federalism

PETER BUßJÄGER

One of the main characteristics of Austrian federalism is the high level of integration between the institutions of the constituent units, the "*Länder*", and the federal government (the Federation), with the latter playing the dominant role. There are a variety of different kinds of relationships between the institutions of the Federation and the *Länder* and a high level of coordination is indispensable. As a result, "cooperation" and "coordination" are the two main keywords to describe Austrian federalism.

A long history of development
Beginning with the birth of the Austrian Federal Constitution in the 1920, during the First Republic (1918 – 1938), there was a strong tendency toward centralization. This tendency reasserted itself at the end of World War Two and persists to the present day, although there have been some modifications of the Federal Constitution which strengthened the legal position of the *Länder*.

During the second half of the 20th Century, the vertical and horizontal instruments of intergovernmental relations in Austria took shape, as did the formal and informal instruments of cooperation and coordination between the *Länder* and the Federation.

The Federation is responsible for any and all modifications of the Federal Constitution and it could even intervene in the constitutional status of the *Länder*. On the other hand, in practice the federal order of government must take into account the political influence of the *Länder* and exercise its power in cooperation with the *Länder*.

Land (state) governors carry out what Austrians call "indirect federal administration". This means that many laws of the Federation are executed at the *Land* level by the *Land* governor on behalf of the appropriate federal authorities. The *Land* governors are bound by the directives of the federal government, but they are still able to exercise significant influence on the way federal laws and regulations are implemented, in practice.

Another source of *Land* governors' power is the fact that they are usually prominent in their political parties and exercise influence, politically, at the federal as well as *Land* level.

Cooperation and Coordination

In Austria, *informal* institutions and actions dominate intergovernmental relations. One reason is that the Austrian upper house, the Federal Council, has no appreciable influence. Lacking an effective upper house to mediate between orders of government Several informal types of cooperation have evolved.

One very important example of this is the *Land* Governors Conference, which involves all the *Länder* in an exercise in "horizontal cooperation". This conference plays a significant role and is an important instrument for coordinating the interests of the *Länder*. The conference takes place twice each year.

In Austria, informal institutions and actions dominate intergovernmental relations. One reason is that the Austrian upper house, the Federal Council, has no appreciable influence. Lacking an effective upper house to mediate between orders of government. Several informal types of cooperation have evolved.

Agreements, according to Art 15a of the Austrian Constitution

The Federation and the *Länder* are entitled to conclude "vertical" agreements with each other. The *Länder* are also allowed to undertake "horizontal" agreements among themselves. Agreements according to Article 15a of the Constitution may deal with all matters within the constitutional responsibilities of the partners. These agreements are probably the most far-reaching legal instrument of cooperative federalism in Austria, but are also a source of controversy. In some instances it does not seem clear that the parties have entered into an agreement entirely of their free will. For example, some commentators criticize one clause of the Austrian Law on Financial Equalisation which stipulates that if the *Länder* do not ratify agreements that relate to the overarching "Austrian pact of fiscal stability", under Constitutional Art 15a, the profit shares which they receive from the federal level will be reduced.

Cooperative federalism

A high degree of integration of key public institutions and organizations is a distinguishing feature of Austrian federalism. The responsibilities of the *Länder* (and as well the municipalities) are often unclear and, to many, the system seems to be clumsy. On the other hand, the involvement of all orders of government (federal, *Land* and municipal) guarantees a certain measure of dynamism in the system.

For historical reasons Austrian federalism is a mix of decentralized, federalist and centralizing tendencies. Although, the main institutions of a federal state exist, in constitutional reality and in practice, they frequently seem to have a pro-forma character.

The upper house Federal Council, is a "political lightweight", while the Conference of the *Land* Governors take on the main job of expressing the *Land* point of view. When the *Land* governors are able to speak with one voice and agree on a common stance towards the federal government the Conference exercises an effective veto power over federal decisions. Indeed, in most cases where the *Länder* object to federal plans unanimously the Federation withdraws those plans.

Usually the Federation and the *Land* governors try to reach a common position through small working groups. Federalism by negotiation in small workings groups means that the parliaments of the Federation and the *Länder* have to execute decisions which were passed without their participation. Many argue that doing things in such a way is not transparent and leads to a weakening of the parliamentary system.

Addressing Social and Regional
Inequalities in Brazil:
Achievements and Ongoing Challenges

MARTA ARRETCHE

In Brazil, no policy output can be understood without taking intergovernmental relations into account.

Subnational governments, particularly local ones, have become the main providers of most services whereas the federal government is in charge of policies related to incomes. Primary education, primary health care, enrollment of welfare recipients, housing, urban development, trash collection, and public transportation are increasingly the responsibility of local governments, while state governments provide secondary education and complex health services as well as water and sewage collection. Social security, unemployment compensation, and welfare payments remain in the hands of the federal government.

It might seem that this is a result of a clear allocation of responsibilities among orders of government, which are independent of each other. That is not the case. It is, rather, the result of evolving and complex intergovernmental relations.

Although constituent units are politically autonomous, their decision-making autonomy – either to collect their own taxes, to spend their own revenues, or to deliver their own policies – is limited by the federal legislation as well as by federal-led, policy-specific national systems.

Hence, federal legislation and policy initiatives provide both incentives to constituent unit governments and constraints on their choices. The critical role of the federal level is the outcome of a historical commitment to nation-wide, uniform policy rules.

Unlike most federations, in Brazil the 5564 local governments have the same legal status as the 26 Brazilian states and the federal district. Moreover, municipalities have emerged as important political players and policy providers as well. Hence, state-level governments tend to have less influence than the federal on local governments' agenda and policy-making.

In fact, the role of state governments has remained loosely defined, even in the most structured realms, such as health and education. This is not to say that state governments have become meaningless. Instead, wherever governors have been able to implement policies that reinforce effectiveness, state-level governments have influenced local government policies.

> Unlike most federations, in Brazil the 5564 local governments have the same legal status as the 26 Brazilian states and the federal district. Moreover, municipalities have emerged as important political players and policy providers as well. Hence, state-level governments tend to have less influence than the federal on local governments' agenda and policy-making.

The influential role the federal government plays, as well as the large number of constitutional provi-sions dealing with constituent units' affairs, does not imply that constituent unit governments merely admi-nister federal laws. Subnational governments still maintain a good deal of autonomy to implement policies in areas of their exclusive responsibility. In addition, they are allowed to implement initiatives going beyond federal requirements – and often do so. A good deal of policy innovation has emerged both from state-level and local governments' initiatives.

A comparison between redistributive and urban development policies can illustrate the impact of intergovernmental relations on policy outcomes.

Health and education policies are implemented by constituent units under a national framework, which earmarks their revenues to specific expenditures. All states and municipalities receive federal conditional transfers earmarked to health and education and expenditures and policy implementation are monitored by state and federal-level agencies. Finally, federal legislation requires local-level participatory policy-specific councils.

Urban development, public transportation, and garbage collection are also de-centralized, but federal regulation in these areas is much looser. As federal trans-fers are not universal spending is federally controlled. As a result, local govern-ments have much larger room to implement policies in these areas their own way.

The outcome is that Brazilian municipalities clearly spend much more on health and education, as opposed to urban development policies, including public transportation. Moreover, horizontal expenditure inequality is much higher in the area of urban development than in education and health.

In sum, federal regulation of constituent units' health and education policies has avoided a *race to the bottom* on redistributive expenditures, has reduced inequality in service provision, and has created arenas for citizens participation in policy monitoring. However, it has resulted in the adverse outcome of crowding out spending on other areas.

In spite of its commitment to nationwide homogeneous policy rules, a great degree of regional inequality has historically marked the Brazilian federation. Economic growth has not been equally distributed, but rather concentrated in the southern and southeast regions. Hence, states' or municipalities' taxable bases vary enormously throughout the country.

As well, subnational units' population size ranges from 800 to 11 million inhabitants among municipalities, and from 400,000 to 40 million among states. The size and wealth of the constituent units is the chief factor determining inequality in self-generated revenue capacities. The fact of the matter is that if Brazil's subnational governments were to count solely on their self-generated tax receipts they would not be able to accomplish the policy tasks for which they are responsible.

A complex system of transfers, whose origins date from the 1946 Constitution, has aimed to address revenue inequality. Constitutional transfers are very important for subnational budgets, providing them with substantial revenues. Their impact varies according to the wealth of each jurisdiction. And so, revenue-sharing does play a genuine redistributive role, although it does not eliminate inequality among regions. There is still substantial variation in subnational governments' spending capacities.

In fact, for the most part, the net effect of transfers favours municipalities and less populated states. Among municipalities, smaller ones receive larger proportional transfers, although poverty is concentrated in metropolitan and larger cities. The rules governing these transfers are based on the outdated assumption that poverty would be concentrated in rural areas and small cities. As a result, despite the redistributive impact of revenue-sharing, many fault the Brazilian fiscal system for failing to provide adequate support to subnational governments. Poorer jurisdictions complain transfers are not enough, while larger ones blame the system for failing to support them to address problems associated with their large concentrations of poor people.

In sum, local governments have become responsible for providing most important public services. Horizontal inequality has been mitigated by the regulatory and redistributive role of the federal government, although not without some adverse effects. The increasing role of local governments might not end up as a zero-sum game with state governments. Indeed, results are mixed. States have loosely defined functions and governors' initiatives are critical both to policy effectiveness and innovation.

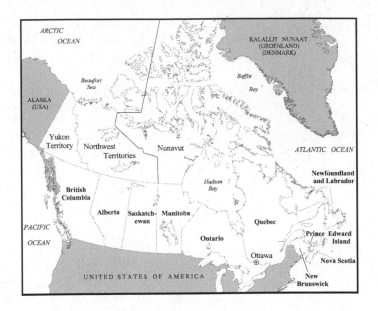

Canada: Evolution at the Margins of the Constitution

MARC-ANTOINE ADAM / JOSÉE BERGERON /
MARIANNE BONNARD[1]

Founded in 1867, Canada was one of the first modern-era federations. The constitutional division of powers between the federal government and the ten provinces – and by extension Canada's three territories – follows the classic dualist model in which each order of government has essentially exclusive responsibility over different sectors, covering both legislative and executive functions.

Following a formula that was established in the first judicial decisions on Canadian federalism, each order of government is sovereign in the domains granted to it by the Constitution. In addition, the federal order of government, like the provincial, is structured according to the British parliamentary system; the government is accountable to the sovereign authority of the legislature.

The founding spirit of the Canadian federation did not envision two orders of government in ongoing mutual relations. In fact, intergovernmental exchanges were rare up until the second half of the 20th century, and were almost exclusively devoted to constitutional questions. However,

---

1. The authors are writing in their personal capacity.

beginning in the 1960s, they started to multiply. Constitutional reform remained an important element, but discussions gradually shifted toward the content of public policy and its tax dimensions.

Since the resounding failures of attempted, major constitutional revision in the late 1980s and early 1990s, the Constitution has almost disappeared from the intergovernmental agenda. At the same time, the number of exchanges has continued to grow, to the point where meetings at all levels (multilateral, bilateral, regional, federal-provincial-territorial, inter-provincial, ministerial, deputy-ministerial, and experts) now number in the hundreds, when not thousands, per year. However, intergovernmental relations remain essentially informal. The Constitution does not provide for a mechanism to support intergovernmental relations, and the courts are reluctant to give legal effect to agreements between governments.

Experts and observers offer many reasons for the expansion of inter-governmental relations. For one, they often cite growing interdependence. Other reasons include:

☐ factors related to the evolution of the role of the state;
☐ electoral imperatives;
☐ the weakness of pan-Canadian political parties;
☐ interest in sharing experiences;
☐ the promotion of national unity;
☐ and even human nature.

Another frequent explanation is that intergovernmental relations com-pensate for the relative rigidity of the Canadian constitutional framework.

Still, the general scope of these explanations does not account for some underlying trends that characterize intergovernmental relations in Canada.

Especially noteworthy is the fact that federal-provincial-territorial forums, which are by far the most numerous of intergovernmental meetings, focus essentially on issues of provincial jurisdiction. In this regard, to understand the dynamics at work, it is essential to consider the central role of finance. After World War II, the federal government, with its larger fiscal resources, was able to become increasingly active in provincial jurisdictions through the use of conditional grants to the provinces. In this way, the federal government played a major role in building the welfare state, even though health care, education and social services are, in principle, provincial responsibilities. This "federal spending power" is not explicitly provided for in the Constitution, but numerous authors support its validity.

Such federal financial intervention in provincial areas of jurisdiction contributed considerably to the development of an intergovernmental dialogue, particularly at the sector level. While at the outset most provinces generally welcomed Ottawa's financial involvement, significant irritants eventually began to appear, especially with the tightening of the public purse strings that marked the 1980s and 1990s. As a result, the provinces sought greater involvement in the elaboration of policies and in determining priorities. This desire for a more active role in relation to the federal government also led to the development of more strategic inter-provincialism. This culminated in the creation, in 2003, of the Council of the Federation, comprising all provincial and territorial premiers. At the same time, intergovernmental meetings involving the country's main aboriginal organizations also began to multiply; these meetings address issues specific to aboriginal communities which often involve both orders of government.

If at the outset strengthened inter-provincialism was motivated by a desire for greater cooperation in the face of federal initiatives, the work of the Council of the Federation rapidly turned to other common issues, such as labour mobility and the environment. Relations within the Council differ from those of federal-provincial-territorial forums. They are charac-terized by a more equal status among the parties, the importance of consensus, and agendas set collectively.

Currently, just as this new provincial leadership is emerging in national governance, the federal government appears to be retreating somewhat from the intergovernmental scene, preferring to negotiate individually with each province or deal directly with individuals.

An assessment of the contribution of intergovernmental relations to the smooth functioning of the federation brings out various perspectives, notably in terms of the interaction between intergovernmental relations and the law.

The perspective of Quebec, the largest province, by territory, and second largest, by population, is particular. One of the four founding provinces, Quebec is distinct by virtue of its francophone majority and civil law system (as opposed to the British tradition common law that pertains in the rest of Canada). Quebec gives much importance to the consti-tutional framework and the idea that intergovernmental practices can serve to bypass this framework is found disturbing. That view is reflected in Quebec's refusal to recognize the federal spending power in areas of provincial jurisdiction. It is also reflected in the way that Quebec seeks structure in intergovernmental relations, for example through inter-governmental agreements that copy the form of legal instruments and a more complex approval process for these agreements.

To varying degrees, the other nine provinces, with common-law traditions, appear less attached to constitutional texts and less inclined to formalize intergovernmental relations. As such, those provinces will often prefer a simple press release, at the conclusion of an intergovernmental conference, over more elaborate formal agreements.

Similarly, from the federal government's perspective, the division of powers must be capable of adapting to societal needs. It therefore prefers not to be bound by intergovernmental relations, invoking instead the need to respect the sovereignty of the federal Parliament. Aboriginal groups, on the other hand, tend to have a perspective closer to that of Quebeckers, despite a very different legal culture; they want to ensure respect for their constitutional rights and hesitate to rely solely on political relations.

These different perspectives and outlooks are further reflected in the diverging assessments of the Canadian federation's current level of centralization, as well as in the variety of opinions on the opportunities for introducing greater diversity, particularly through asymmetrical arrangements. The ability of federal-provincial-territorial dynamics to promote innovation in public policy is also a controversial topic in Canada. From the provincial perspective, conditional federal grants appear to discourage provincial innovation. Ottawa's view is that this system allows good ideas tried out at the provincial level to be replicated at the national level.

Similarly, from the federal government's perspective, the division of powers must be capable of adapting to societal needs. It therefore prefers not to be bound by intergovernmental relations, invoking instead the need to respect the sovereignty of the federal Parliament.

Other divisions exist, particularly between intergovernmental relations specialists, who attach considerable importance to process, and sector policy specialists, who focus on results above all. External observers appear critical of the lack of transparency in intergovernmental relations; many demand greater involvement of parliamentarians and the inclusion of new players such as cities and non-governmental organizations. Intergovernmental relations insiders respond by underlining the fundamental role of provinces as mediators of interests in a federal system and, more generally, the role of elected governments in a representative democracy. In that way, the initial debate over the contribution of intergovernmental relations leads to other debates on the nature and culture of federalism in Canada.

EU: Intergovernmental Relations
in a Supranational Federation

NICOLAS LEVRAT

The European Union (EU) could be described as a supranational organization, with features both of an international organization, and, increasingly, of a federal system. This dynamic is important: the EU is in permanent evolution, both in terms of size and institutional regime.

The EU[1] was born in the 1950s with six Member States (which we can consider to be the EU's constituent units) and with a population of less than 200 million. It then evolved, to nine "constituent units" in 1972, 10 in 1980, 12 in 1986, 15 in 1995, 25 in 2004.

As of 2007, the EU is made up of 27 constituent entities and is home to about 500 million inhabitants. Several European countries are currently candidates to join the EU, which may thus further enlarge in the future.

---

1. The legal and institutional situation is actually much more complex. Officially, the EU was only instituted in 1993, as a new system encompassing the 3 "Communities" created in the 1950s. The latest evolution, which may enter into force in 2010 will see the disappearance of the Economic Community, to be replaced by the European Union. However and for the sake of the present publication, we will always refer to the EU, notwithstanding institutional and legal subtleties.

From an institutional perspective, the EU is based on three international Treaties, two concluded among six States in the 1950s, and one among 12 States in 1992.

Since the mid-1980s, the institutional framework and the relations between and among the constituent units (that, is, the member states) have been in constant restructuring, with frequent revisions of the Treaties, including a failed attempt to create a new EU based on a "Constitutive Treaty". The most recent and all-encompassing revised Treaty (the Lisbon Treaty), is now going through a ratification process in each member State. 25 out of 27 have already voted in favour of the Lisbon Treaty, which, however, must gain unanimous approval.

Intergovernmental relations within the EU have to be assessed in the context of this evolution

Since its founding, the dominant trend has been for the EU, itself, to replace horizontal "international relations" between States. In EU jargon this is called "intergovernmental relations" by supranational institutions and procedures. For the sake of analysis, we can identify three types of intergovernmental relations in the EU:

☐ classic "international relations" type of interaction between member states;

☐ relations structured within formal institutions (which for the sake of argument can be characterized as "federal" ones); and

☐ other modes of interaction, either formal or informal, between members states or between them and the EU (that is "federal") authorities.

Intergovernmental relations as classic international relations

Since the EU is not a State, its constituent units (which *are* sovereign States) remain fully competent in all matters not attributed to the EU by the founding Treaties. In these matters, member states continue practicing classic international relations, either in a purely horizontal fashion or through other European organizations – such as the Council of Europe, the OECD, the OSCE or NATO.

For example, most fiscal issues lie outside the authority of the EU, and are thus left for national governments to deal with in bilateral administrative arrangements (under OECD guidance). This lack of fiscal power at the EU level is particularly significant for the practice of intergovernmental relations with the EU. The EU has a limited budget (less than 1% of its members' collective GDP) and thus has limited capacity to use its "spending power" in areas where it does not formally have responsibility.

Intergovernmental relations as practiced through EU institutions

The EU's original institutional framework did not put in place a true government at the European level. The central institution was the Council of Ministers, composed of delegates (Ministers or Ambassadors) of the governments of the member states. This "confederal" design ensured a very effective form of representation of the governments of the "units". This had the effect of increasingly marginalizing intergovernmental relations, which tended to take place outside this official setting. However, developments both in formal institutional terms and in practice, have reinforced the supranational character of the EU.

Consequently, from a system in which governments of the "units" remained the main – if not the sole – holders of power, the EU gradually adopted an institutional character more familiar to democratic federal countries. Despite significant differences, the Council of Ministers now appears to some extent as a second Chamber of the legislative power (comparable to the German *Bundesrat*). Meanwhile, the European Parliament, whose members are directly elected, may be compared to the first Chamber of the legislative branch. For its part, the EU Commission increasingly presents itself as a European government. It is politically responsible to and formally chosen by the European Parliament, even though national governments maintain a major influence on its composition.

Thus, the direct representation of national interests, which was once the dominant mode of relations within the EU, is gradually being sidelined. We are now witnessing the evolution of various modes of both horizontal and vertical intergovernmental relations outside institutional channels – again, along the lines of fully-fledged federations.

A major intergovernmental trend in the EU derives from the impact of the gradual extension of EU areas of responsibility, replacing national ones. In federal (or quasi-federal) member states (Austria, Belgium, Germany, Italy, Spain, and to some extent Portugal and the UK) this implies the transfer to the EU, of a number of responsibilities which – in the domestic context – lie within the sphere of the constituent units of these national federations (the *Länder*, regions, autonomous communities, etc.). As a consequence, these constituent units also wish to be involved at the EU level, sometimes in complex ways, captured by the expression "multi-level governance".

In 1993, this tendency was translated into two institutional innovations.

First, the creation of the Committee of the Regions, a consultative EU organ, in which constituent units of the EU, the member States, delegate elected representatives of their local and regional authorities, including, for federal or quasi-federal members states, their own constituent units.

Second, the EU Treaty henceforth formally authorizes the members states who so wish to be represented within the Council of Minister by a member of the government of one of their constituent units. This latest evolution leads to a strengthening of vertical intergovernmental relations within these Member States, since a single regional Minister is responsible for defending the national interest of the whole country at the EU level.

Emerging "informal" intergovernmental relations which are neither "classic" nor "institutional"

Alongside those trends that are clearly linked to the evolution of the institutional design of the EU's "federal regime", informal channels of intergovernmental relations have also emerged. They involve both the EU "constituent units" or member States and their own constituent units (*Länder,* etc). Those mechanisms are both horizontal and vertical.

Vertical intergovernmental relations follow both a top-down and a bottom-up dynamic. The first results are efforts by the European Commission to develop relations with the governments of member States or their constituent units (such as German *Länder* or Spanish autonomous communities), in order to ensure the effective implementation of EU laws or policies. Pursuant to EU law, the Commission is politically responsible to the European Parliament for the proper implementation of EU law and policies. However, the *means* of implementation rest solely with the national or sub-national governments. There is a very small EU "federal" administration, of less than 40,000 civil servants. Consequently, the Commission must develop relations with national or sub-national governments to ensure that EU norms and program are properly developed and applied "on the ground".

While it plays no formal role in implementation, the European Commission plays a very central role in the EU law-making process, since legislative proposals may only emanate from the Commission. Thus, in addition to their formal representation within EU institutions, governments of the member states, or their regions, develop important – bottom-up – informal channels of influence directed at the Commission.

Horizontal intergovernmental relations also play a significant role within the EU. Indeed, some member states seem to favour bilateral relations between their governments (often called Summits), in which political declarations are adopted and transmitted to the EU "federal" institutions.

Interestingly, sub-national entities (*Länder,* regions, etc.) rather prefer multilateral relations, often through associations which adopt common positions that are then forwarded to the same EU "federal" level. These "horizontal" relations thus end up having a vertical dimension as well.

We must note one final substantial aspect: member states sometimes develop institutionalized relationship, even formalized through binding legal agreements, which are later incorporated into the EU "federal" institutional patterns, through Treaty revisions. For instance, the "Schengen" agreements (which involve common rules of access to EU territory) originated from a form of horizontal intergovernmental relations in the late 1980s. That took place before the matter was officially transferred to the EU in 1997, through the Amsterdam Treaty.

A distinct process was initiated by the European Commission in 2000 with the "Open Method of Coordination", according to which constituent units, or member states, with or without their own constituent units, cooperate outside of the scope of formal EU responsibilities, on the basis of soft governance mechanisms (benchmarking, for example). Such a process acts as a substitute for direct EU ("federal") action, despite a certain measure of activism on the part of the Commission.

***

In conclusion, it appears that within the EU, intergovernmental relations are in a somewhat paradoxical relationship with the institutional evolution of the federal (EU) level. Traditional intergovernmental relations are progressively being replaced by a strengthening of the institutions at the federal level. However, when, for political reasons, new responsibilities or procedures cannot be instituted at the federal level, new modes of intergovernmental relations – such as the Open method of coordination – are developed, often jointly by the constituent units, the Member States, and the federal authority, the Commission.

Federal Governance in Germany Between Party Politics and Administrative Networks

ROLAND LHOTTA / JULIA VON BLUMENTHAL

German federalism is usually described as "intrastate federalism", featuring highly developed "executive federalism" with far-reaching cooperation between levels of government.

The need for intense collaboration between levels of government is fuelled by Germany's system of power sharing based on a functional distribution of competences. While most legislative powers are bestowed on the national government, the administrative power – including the implementation of federal laws – is concentrated at the subnational level of the *Länder* (the states).

The German second chamber of the national parliament, the *Bundesrat* (the "senate" or upper house), plays the role of defending the administrative interests of the *Länder* through its veto power and involvement in national governance. The *Bundesrat* is an assembly of representatives from the *Länder* governments which provides for the continuous participation of sub-national governments in the policy making process on the national level.

Due to this intricate, intertwined system, cooperation with the *Länder* governments is essential for any national government. Nearly every important legislative act of the national government and its supporting governing majority in the *Bundestag*, the popularly elected "lower house", needs to gain the backing of the *Bundesrat*. Federal encroachments on the *implementation* of federal laws – in order to secure uniform administration of federal laws throughout the federation – generated the significant proliferation of obligatory support of the *Bundesrat*. This, in turn, became the main power resource of the second chamber and a trigger for intergovernmental cooperation.

When there is a different political party majority in the *Bundesrat* than in the *Bundestag* the national government finds itself obliged to curb any high flying policy ambitions. However, even in times of concurrent majorities in both chambers, the *Länder* influence through the *Bundesrat* is remarkably great. The leaders of the 16 *Länder* governments, the *Ministerpräsidenten*, continuously seek power and a participatory role at the national level. "Playing the Bundesrat card" can mean exploiting the second chamber for party politics, as well as for *Länder*-specific policy preferences.

A second motive for the close cooperation between both levels of government is the doctrine, enshrined in the German constitution, of equal – or, since the constitutional amendment of 1994, "equivalent" – living conditions throughout the country.

There is a significant degree of horizontal cooperation between *Länder* governments in Germany leading to a high level of uniformity even in policy fields of exclusive *Länder* competence. These collaborations reach far back into the times before the Federal Republic of Germany was founded.

In 1949, ministers of education from the western occupation zones met and constituted the *Standing Conference of the Ministers of Education and Cultural Affairs of the Länder in the Federal Republic of Germany (KMK)*. The *KMK*, with its secretariat and its regular meetings on the ministerial as well as on different administrative levels, still serves as the major forum for the joint development of Germany's educational system. Notwithstanding this, it is also known as an institution incapable of effective decision-making, since its strictly consensual character inhibits radical and timely policy changes.

Other ministerial conferences, such as the *Conference of the Länder Ministers of the Interior (IMK)* or the *Conference of the Ministers of Economics*, are less well staffed, operate mostly without public attention and provide more efficient means of horizontal collaboration. In addition, they also serve as fora for vertical policy coordination. Federal ministers more often than not attend the conferences of *Länder* ministers as guests. In some cases they even serve as regular members, such as in the *Conferences of Ministers of Agriculture, Spatial Planning, and Consumer Protection*.

Following the 1969 constitutional reform several new bodies of collaborative decision-making between national and *Länder* governments were set up, not all of which outlasted the zenith of political planning, in Germany, in the 1970s. In particular, the so-called *Gemeinschaftsaufgaben* (joint-tasks) – a corner stone of the constitutionalized cooperation system – quickly proved to be an unsuitable tool and were finally restricted, or eliminated, in the last constitutional reform in 2006.

Today, the practice of intergovernmental relations in Germany is characterized by a complex system of formal institutions and informal fora, in which representatives from the political and administrative spheres meet regularly, exchange experiences, adjust administrative practices and develop policy proposals.

As one might expect, the major challenges for German federalism and its intergovernmental relations have resulted from German unification and European integration. Both required considerable adaptation on the part of the federal and *Länder* administrations.

With regard to the structures and procedures of intergovernmental relations, the process of German unification has now been successfully completed. Administrative networks are formed by experts without regard to their own regional origins. The *Ministerpräsidenten* of the five eastern *Länder* and Berlin still hold separate meetings, but the East-West divide has ceased to play a decisive role – apart from financial issues where the new *Länder* still fight jointly for additional subsidies from the federal government and the European Union and for favourable conditions within the system of horizontal fiscal equalization.

Many thought European integration, with its shift of responsibilities to the supra-national level of the EU, would be the last nail in the coffin of *Länder* autonomy. However, the development proved to be less dramatic. The new cooperation procedures of Article 23 of the German constitution, which deals with the transfer of powers to the European Union and the consequences for the distribution of competences within the German system, actually offered new avenues for *Länder* influence and policy participation at the European level. Moreover, the *Länder* have displayed significant institutional adaptability and flexibility in dealing with the contingencies of cooperation in a multi-level system. Intergovernmental relations have become more complex and sophisticated, but also offer new opportunities for the *Länder* to represent their interests at the EU level.

Today, the future of intergovernmental relations in Germany largely depends on the role of the political parties. To date, intergovernmental relations have largely been driven by the rationale of professional expertise and competence. If, however, partisan politics start to seriously encroach on the networks of administrative experts, intergovernmental relations in Germany might lose some of their problem-solving and conflict-managing capacities.

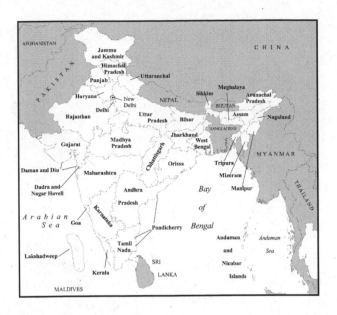

Intergovernmental Relations in India

M.P SINGH / REKHA SAXENA

India was the first country in the Afro-Asian world to adopt a parliamentary federal constitution, in 1949-50. Federalization was a product of the combined processes of devolution from the centre to the British Indian provinces, and the integration of five hundred-odd princely Indian states through diplomatic negotiation and military action.

British colonial rule in India, since at least the mid-nineteenth century, had established a fairly institutionalized process of interaction between the "center" (the national or federal government, first in Calcutta and subsequently in New Delhi), on the one hand, and the Governors and the Chief Commissioner's provinces on the other. Alongside, the British Imperial Viceroy, at the centre, and the British diplomatic agents called Regents, in princely states, also had well-oiled channels of communication. (The same representative of the British Crown in India doubled as the Governor General and the Viceroy.)

The first federal scheme introduced by the Government of India Act (1935) provided for an Inter-Provincial Council, but the central part of the Act remained in abeyance because of the reluctance of the princely rulers to join the proposed federation. Congress Party provincial ministries, under the 1935 Act, were beholden to the "high command" of the Indian National Congress and the Governors were under direct bureaucratic control of the Governor General.

While the 1950 Constitution of India empowers the Union (or central/ federal) government in significant ways, as the authoritative locus of policy initiation and coordination and with overriding legislative and executive powers over the state governments, intergovernmental relations have become considerably transformed since the period of the Congress party's dominance in New Delhi and in most of the states. The emergence of a federal multi-party system and divided governments since 1989, in a regionally and culturally diverse society makes the enterprise of governance today heavily contingent on meaningful and effective intergovernmental interactions.

The neo-liberal capitalist reforms undertaken since 1991, combined with global and regional integration of the Indian economy, make intergovernmental interactions all the more necessary, in both policy development and service delivery.

The typical pattern of intergovernmental relations in the era of the Congress party's dominance was to settle matters across the table of transactions among the highest executives of the ruling party and the Union Government cabinet, which represented all major states and communities. Both were dominated by the federal Prime Minister.

The Nehru government avoided establishing the Inter-State Council (ISC) mandated by Article 263 of the Constitution and, instead, set up the National Development Council (NDC) and a series of National Councils in several policy areas. All these bodies were intergovernmental in representation. While the NDC was used for intergovernmental approval of the five-year plans prepared by the national Planning Commission, in consultation with Union ministries and state governments, the various national councils were used as the sounding boards for nationally laid down policies.

More frequent were *ad hoc* chief ministers'/ministers'/secretaries' conferences on topical policy issues and problems, chaired by the Prime Minister, Union ministers or Union secretaries (senior civil servants). These were convened by the center, from time to time. Thus "executive federalism" had been, until fairly recently, the typical mode of intergovernmental relations in India, as it still is in a number of other parliamentary federal systems.

The advent in 1989 of the first multi-party coalitional minority government caused the the Inter-State Council to be set up for the first time. This was in pursuit of an election promise to activate federal institutions. However, this constitutional intergovernmental forum has not really come into its own, although it has done some useful work in promoting dialogue on the future shape of Indian federalism.

The principal explanation for this state of affairs may be that the federal coalition governments have commonly included such large numbers of regional and national parties (ranging from eight or fifteen to twenty four) that they represent a fairly wide federal consensus.

Federal power sharing has brought even sociologically and ideologically small parties, groups and tendencies into ruling coalitions. Powerful regional satraps have preferred to stay in state politics as Chief Ministers or party bosses, sending their juniors into the federal coalition cabinets, but "with strings attached". This pattern of coalition governments helped to prevent serious jurisdictional conflicts between the Union government and those of the states.

Consensual coalition cabinets also overshadowed intergovernmental fora such as the ISC, the NDC and Union-state conferences, which remained of formal interest only for those parties and state governments that were not part of Union coalition governments. While these developments have allowed regional forces freer play and articulated the federal features of the Constitution, there are problems that we must note.

The constitutional principles of individual responsibility of ministers to the Prime Minister and collective responsibility of the cabinet to the Parliament have become strained almost to the breaking point on occasions. Coherent policy initiation and coordination have become difficult to sustain. These problems might have been avoided had there been a nationally integrated party system at the federal level in India, as is the case, more or less, in Australia and Canada.

It is notable that the Presidential Order establishing the ISC did not give all the powers that the Constitution had envisaged for it. The Order excluded clause A of Article 263 of India's Constitution, which would have charged the ISC with the duty of " inquiring into and advising on disputes which may have arisen between the States." The absence of this power weakens the political processes of settling inter-state and intergovernmental disputes and contributes to an overload of responsibility on the Union executive and, ultimately, on the judiciary. Ironically, there are some other instances where the full potential of the constitutional provisions for political and adjudicatory settlement of inter-state disputes and conflicts have not been fully utilized.

One such area is inter-state river water disputes, where the Constitution provides for political settlement through negotiations between the affected states or through adjudication by a tribunal appointed by the Union government (all the while, preferably keeping the Supreme Court out of the loop). The Inter-State River Water Disputes Act (1956), enacted under this article of the Constitution, does not provide for a binding award by such a Tribunal. Failing solution by the political or tribunal routes, the matter has often ended up in the Supreme Court.

Another instance of the underuse of constitutional provisions is Article 307 of the Constitution, which empowers the Parliament to provide, by law, for the appointment of an autonomous Inter-State Trade and Commerce Commission. The purpose of this body is to ensure free trade throughout the territory of India and to harmonize restrictions on trade imposed by the Parliament or the state legislatures. Ironically, again, despite India being one of the largest domestic markets in Asia, no such commission has yet been appointed, notwithstanding the National Commission to Review the Working of the Constitution (NCRWC) (2002) recommending in favour of it.

The NCRWC chaired by Justice M.N Venkatachailah aptly underlined the need for making intergovernmental fora more effective. The present Centre State Relations Commission chaired by Justice M. N Punchi would do well to look into this issue and come up with appropriate recommendations to deal with the constitutional and political problems outlined above.

Since the acceleration of neoliberal capitalist reforms, starting in 1991, a series of autonomous regulatory authorities have been established under Acts of Parliament, in various sectors of the national economy. These correspond to parallel state agencies that deal with matters within their exclusive state jurisdiction.

One often hears two kinds of views about intergovernmental relations, in India. One view is that the intergovernmental mechanisms in use have served Indian federal system reasonably well. However, a more frequently articulated perspective suggests that there is an imperative to make intergovernmental relations and broader interactions for governance to be *more inclusive, interactive and accountable.*

These questions need to be examined in the context of the new challenges of federalization and globalization. These macro changes have a significant impact on the capability of the Indian federal system to cope with the pressing problems of accommodating diversity and dealing with the threats posed by terrorism, nuclear weapons, global warming and climate change.

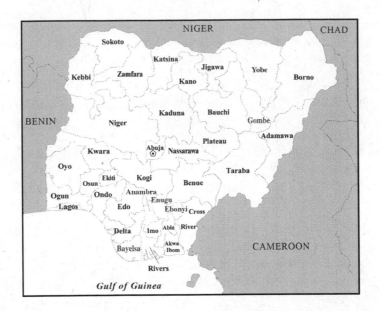

Nigeria: Intergovernmental Relations in a Highly Centralized Federation

EGHOSA E. OSAGHAE

Nigeria belongs to the genre of federations which began as unitary or quasi-unitary systems, but later disaggregated into an ever-increasing number of constituent units. The country's complex ethnic and religious diversity was a major factor in this process. From three regions in 1954, when the country first adopted a federal constitution, the number increased to four in 1963. Under military rule, the regions were abrogated and replaced first with 12 states in 1967, 19 states in 1976, 21 states in 1987, 30 states in 1991 and, finally, 36 states in 1996 (to these should be added the Federal Capital Territory (FCT) of Abuja which operates as a 'federal state').

The military also introduced local government reforms which sought to make local government an autonomous, third order of the federal system. Although state governments have resisted the attempts by the federal government to take control of local governments, the number of local councils created by the federal government has increased, over the years, from 444 in 1976 to 774 in 1996.

The 1999 Constitution, according to which the post-military civilian democracy has operated, defines Nigeria as a federation consisting of the federal government, 36 states and the FCT, and 774 local government councils.

Following from this, the Nigerian federation may be described as a three-tier (federal-state-local) system, though in practice, and to the extent that local authorities are subordinate to state governments in important respects, the federal government and state governments constitute the main orders of government.

By far the most prominent feature of intergovernmental relations in Nigeria is the dominance of the federal government in the executive, legislative and judicial spheres. One good illustration of this is the constitutional division of legislative powers, which under the 1999 constitution, allocates 68 items to the exclusive (federal) legislative list and 12 to the concurrent list which, in almost all cases, limits state jurisdiction to federal benevolence.

Federal government dominance is further reflected in the fiscal arrangements that not only place control over oil (which provides over 80 per cent of total national revenue) but all other major taxes in the hands of federal authorities. These arrangements also make federal government allocations to states and municipalities contingent on state and local government performance.

Other indicators of federal dominance include:

☐ The absolute control by federal authorities of police and security;

☐ The determinate roles of the National Judicial Commission and other central bodies in the appointment of state judges and other state officials; and

☐ Federal control of party politics and electoral system.

As well, since the return to civilian democracy in 1999, the awesome powers of the federal government have been demonstrated in even more dramatic ways.

To date, the federal government has declared a state of emergency that involves the removal of the government and appointment of a federal administrator in two states, Plateau and Ekiti, where law and order were judged to have broken down. In addition, the National Assembly, as the federal legislature is known, has taken over the legislative functions of states in one instance (Anambra) and threatened to do so in another (Ogun).

The overbearing power of the federal government might very well be one of the inevitable consequences of the origins of the federal system, through disaggregation, and the fact that the constituent units are creations of the federal government. It was, however, accentuated by prolonged periods of military rule.

The military ruled for 30 of the country's first 40 years of independence, 1966-1979, 1984-1999. The military organizational principles of unity of command, centralization and hierarchical authority were key factors in the ascendancy of the federal government to the 'master' position. Added to those factors, based on the character of military rule in general, were two others. First there was the military's pursuit of national unity in an effort, ostensibly, to suppress the centrifugal forces that led to the civil war (1967-70). And, second, there was the advent of oil wealth after the civil war which provided the wherewithal for the federal government to take over responsibilities that previously belonged to the states. Although military rule ended in 1999, the influence of 'military federalism' remains strong.

In addition to the factors cited above there is the unavoidable fact that there is a class of military-influenced politicians who have been the beneficiaries and 'gatekeepers' of fiscal and political centralization.

Finally, there are three other factors responsible for the Nigerian system of federally skewed intergovernmental relations:

☐ The regulation of political parties is an exclusive federal legislative matter and requires parties to be national in character and headquartered in the federal capital Abuja;

☐ The electoral system affords the federal government ample room for influencing who controls power in the states; and

☐ Since the return to civilian democracy in 1999, there have been a series of centralizing economic and governance reforms, implemented under the direction of the federal government at the behest of the World Bank and other international development creditors and partners.

One consequence of the skewed intergovernmental terrain, not surprisingly, has been a struggle by the states to regain autonomous grounds lost to the centre under military rule. For many states the enormous powers wielded by the four regional governments of the pre-military period remain a reference point.

The states are in a constant struggle to reconfigure the structure of fiscal relations to give states (and localities) a larger share of the federation's centrally collected revenues. The oil rich states of the Niger Delta are especially concerned about this, but they are not alone.

Multiparty democracy and landmark judicial decisions have afforded some major gains for the states, although control of local government remains a sore point.

At the level of horizontal intergovernmental relations, although state-state relations have mostly followed the lines of old regional affiliations (which have been reinforced by the division of the country into six political zones), structures such as the Governors Forum and Forum of Speakers of State Assemblies have strengthened interstate cooperation. Local government councils have also pursued a cooperative agenda through national bodies such as the Association of Local Governments of Nigeria, the National Councillors' Forum and the National Union of Local Government Employees.

Vertical intergovernmental relations, especially involving federal ministers and state commissioners, tax agencies and similar organizations, have served to entrench the dominance of federal authorities, although, at least superficially, they have been cooperative and harmonious.

Not shown: Prince Edward Islands

Intergovernmental Relations in South Africa – Growing Pains of a New System or Multi-level Government at the Crossroads?

DEREK POWELL

Since the adoption of the Constitution in 1996, intergovernmental relations in South Africa have exhibited three contrasting tendencies: the national government's dominance, strong devolution to *local* government, and growing use of statutory structures to manage intergovernmental relations. So far the process of intergovernmental relations has helped contain the pressures of a new democracy trying to build a more equal society. However, persistent and extreme poverty and inequality have led many to question the effectiveness of South Africa's multi-level government.

The Constitution established elected national, provincial and local spheres of government, allocated powers and responsibilities to each and set the framework for intergovernmental relations. There are nine provinces and two hundred and eighty three municipalities. Provinces participate in national law-making through the National Council of Provinces, the second chamber of Parliament.

All spheres of government are duty-bound to conduct intergovernmental relations in ways that build cooperation, avoid litigation, resolve conflict, and promote the interests of the country as a whole.

The national Parliament has also enacted legislation on intergovernmental relations and dispute resolution. In practice, relations between and among governments, at all levels, are conducted both through the formal institutions created by this legislation and through informal contacts.

But the various spheres of government – local, provincial and national – do not participate as equals. There are strong incentives for the national government to play a dominant role and the opportunities for sub-national governments to negotiate fairer terms of engagement are more limited.

The national government controls the main policy, fiscal and economic levers of the state, including the major tax and revenue instruments. Provinces and municipalities must implement national policies that seek to achieve equity, and redress the realization of basic human rights. Their main service delivery responsibilities are largely funded through intergovernmental transfers.

National targets for poverty eradication and growth are the focus of planning and budgeting for all governments and the formulae that determine the division of revenue between different orders of government are heavily weighted to these targets. Consequently, intergovernmental discussions and transactions largely focus on progress *vis-à-vis* national targets. The subnational units' expenditure performances' are evaluated in the light of these national targets and little attention is paid to sub-national priorities not linked to national priorities. With the exception of the largest cities, subnational governments have limited scope to fund priorities that are not on the national register. Several provincial premiers have expressed a concern that provinces are merely the delivery agents of the national government.

In addition, party politics moulds intergovernmental relations around the national political agenda. All three levels of government are principally elected on the party-list system. With the main political parties in the country dominant at all three levels, provincial and local politics mirror national politics.

The ruling African National Congress is the majority party throughout government - with a near two thirds majority in Parliament and control of all nine provinces and most municipalities. Until recently, the President of the ANC appointed candidates for provincial premier and municipal mayor.

Political interference in the appointment of public servants and procurement, corruption and patronage are growing problems, particularly in local government. In 2007, a bitter contest over leadership of the ANC split the party into two factions. One faction formed a new party. These divisions still run deep in government and in some cases have paralyzed intergovernmental relations. The new ANC leadership wants more state intervention in the economy, which will further reinforce national control of intergovernmental relations.

Decentralization to local government is a countervailing trend in South Africa. The constitution and national policy give local government a strong developmental mandate and significant powers. The six largest cities are home to the majority of the population and the major economic centres in the country. National policy further requires that the integrated development plans of municipalities guide all state expenditure plans.

A statutory association represents organized local government in inter-governmental forums at all levels. Such institutions provide an opportunity for subnational governments to assert their interests. In practice, however, national concerns generally prevail.

In line with national goals intergovernmental structures have placed a high priority on municipal performance in the provision of services such as water and sanitation), measured against national poverty eradication targets, and on financial accountability. Nonetheless, organized local government has used intergovernmental processes successfully to lobby for increases to local government's share of revenue, and as for stronger checks on unfunded mandates and restraint in policy proposals that have an adverse impact on municipal revenues.

> Decentralization to local government is a countervailing trend in South Africa. The constitution and national policy give local government a strong developmental mandate and significant powers.

The relationship between some big cities and their provinces is especially difficult. Contestation over provincial functions, notably housing and public transport, is commonplace. Cities want control of these provincial functions to manage their built environments more effectively. Provinces are threatened by the economic might of cities and fear losing power through further devolution.

In 2005, the national Parliament enacted the Intergovernmental Relations Framework Act to establish the main structures for intergovernmental interaction at the executive level. At the same time, the Act established alternative dispute resolution procedures. The Act included protocols as an incentive for the different orders of government to negotiate the terms of cooperation. These protocols have been used to manage the after-effects of provincial boundary changes and to address problems in the education sector in one province, but their usage is not widespread.

Dispute resolution is predicated on the orders of government taking rea-sonable steps to resolve intergovernmental disputes, before resorting to the courts. The ruling party's dominance means that most disputes are resolved through party structures. Opportunities for intergovernmental negotiations across party lines are limited and tend to be antagonistic, not cooperative.

The South African system of intergovernmental relations has evolved rapidly in a short time. Poverty, inequality and unemployment are serious threats to stability and lead the reform agenda. Now, the country is in the midst of a recession because of the global financial crisis and unemployment has increased (the time of writing is late-2009). There is severe pressure on all orders of government to address the plight of the poor.

In 2009, a new government took office, nationally, with a mandate for change. Change of some kind is a certainty. In the future, intergovernmental relations will likely be marked by increased national assertiveness, and possibly more fundamental reforms to South Africa's system of multi-level government.

Intergovernmental Relations in Spain

MARÍA JESÚS GARCÍA MORALES /
XAVIER ARBÓS MARÍN

Spain has been a politically decentralized State for a little over 30 years. The Constitution of 1978 brought democracy and political decentralization at the same time, after a very centralist State was dismantled. The new Spanish State, commonly referred to as "State of the Autonomies", comprising a central government and 17 territorial bodies known as Autonomous Communities, constitutes the longest experience in democracy in Spanish history.

Intergovernmental relations are not accounted for in the Constitution, but they are a decisive element in the political decentralization process. In Spain, cooperation mechanisms have taught something as important as the need to share problems and seek solutions between a central government – accustomed to deciding unilaterally – and Autonomous Communities.

Over the years, intergovernmental relations have been characterised by three main features.

☐ One, they are almost entirely vertical relationships (between the central government and the Autonomous Communities);

☐ Two, there is almost no formalized cooperation on a horizontal level (between and among the Autonomous Communities);

☐ And three, there is no intergovernmental forum institutionalized at the highest level. Nonetheless, the European integration process, the reforming of the Statutes of Autonomy – the institutional norms of Autonomous Communities – and the creation of a prime ministers' conference, known as "Conference of Presidents" in 2004 are indicative of change.

Since the beginning of the "State of the Autonomies", cooperation mechanisms between the central government and the Autonomous Communities have been developed multilaterally and bilaterally, but the most common form of relationship is clearly multilateral. The Sectoral Conferences, the most important cooperation instrument in Spain, are multilateral, as are the joint agreements and plans that come out of them.

The Conferences bring together the minister in the central government and his/her counterparts in the governments of the Autonomous Communities in order to discuss draft legislation, to co-ordinate the participation of Autonomous Communities in European affairs, and, above all, to allocate funds from the central government to the Autonomous Communities.

Cooperation between the central government and the Autonomous Communities is largely centred on funding, especially with regard to sectors that are under the exclusive jurisdiction of the Autonomous Communities, such as social services. Sectoral Conferences are convened and chaired by the central government and they operate on an unequal basis. Many of them lack a stable organizational structure and, in some cases, they are highly politicized. As a consequence, there have only rarely been instances of true participation by the Autonomous Communities in national affairs.

In addition to multilateral cooperation, the central government and each one of the Autonomous Communities cooperate in what are called Bilateral Commissions. These are not a formalized forum for high-level political dealings. Their primary function is to settle disputes between the central government and each one of the Autonomous Communities. If a dispute arises due to a law set forth by the central government or by a Community, either of the two parties may request that the Bilateral Commission convene – in order to use political negotiation, and to avoid bringing the case before the Constitutional Court. The Commission is a distinctive conflict resolution process that has made it possible to significantly reduce territorial conflicts.

The most recent Statutes of Autonomy, following Catalonia's 2006 lead, have integrated within them the role of the Bilateral Commissions. This demonstrates a political desire to strengthen the bilateral component of relationships between the central government and the Autonomous Communities, a desire often brought about by dissatisfaction with the way multilateral instruments have operated. However, the outcome of this new formalized "bilateralness" and its effect on multilateral mechanisms is still unknown.

Horizontal cooperative mechanisms are very weak, which is shown by the small number of agreements between Autonomous Communities. Cooperation between Autonomous Communities has been based on informal relationship mechanisms, while the few existing agreements between Autonomous Communities are signed between neighbouring Communities.

There are no agreements in which all or even most Autonomous Communities take part. That is to be expected, since there are no sectoral Conferences that engage the Autonomous Communities, without the central government. Nor is there anything on the order of "Conference of Presidents", exclusively for heads of Autonomous Community governments. Were they to exist, such institutions would act as meeting points where Autonomous Communities would be able to exchange information, discuss joint activities and agree upon common stances.

In fact, though, the Autonomous Communities have preferred to interact with the central government. It is now, perhaps, time that they learn how to interact with one another – with the aim of improving the way in which they carry out their responsibilities and to better defend their common interests *vis-à-vis* the central government.

One can, even now, perceive some signs of change. An important new event has been instituted: the Meetings among the six Autonomous Communities, whose new Statutes were approved in 2006 or later. They are: Comunidad Valenciana, Catalonia, Balearic Islands, Andalusia, Aragon and Castille and Leon. In addition, the European integration process may be an excellent stimulus for horizontal cooperation, in that it forces Autonomous Communities to work together to participate in European affairs.

As well in 2004 there was a Conference of Presidents bringing together, for the first time, the Prime Minister of Spain and the heads of Autonomous Community governments. This is the most important intergovernmental initiative in Spain, yet it still does not operate on a regular basis.

The creation of such a Conference represents a symptom of institutional normality. Previously, in Spain, there was no official forum where the heads of government were able to meet. Moreover, the Conference signifies an important opportunity to introduce a more coherent

> In fact, thought, the Autonomous Communities have preferred to interact with the central government. It is now, perhaps, time that they learn how to interact with one another – with the aim of improving the way in which they carry out their responsibilities and to better defend their common interests *vis-à-vis* the central government.

approach to the system of intergovernmental relations, since in the "State of the Autonomies", there has not been a general body at the highest political level to address State issues and to promote the work of the Sectoral Conferences.

Still, the Conference of Presidents in Spain is vertical, so it may reproduce problems already found in the Sectoral Conferences. One could argue that the presence of the central government hinders multilateral coordination among all of the Autonomous Communities.

In 2008, there was a proposal to convene a Conference of Presidents solely among Autonomous Communities, which could be a good complement to the 2004 Conference, because it would stimulate a level of cooperation between Autonomous Communities that has not existed until now.

Intergovernmental relations in Spain currently find themselves in a time of change. The behaviour of political actors can be difficult to change, but the process of European integration, the new Statutes of Autonomy and the institutionalization of the Conference of Presidents may mark a turning point in intergovernmental relations in Spain that only time will confirm.

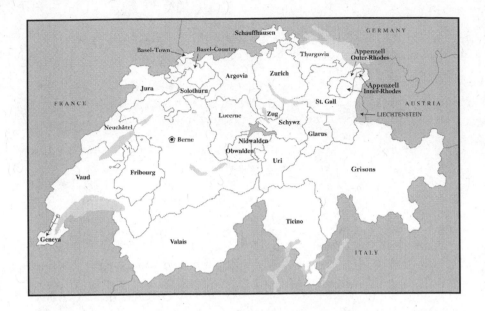

The Latest Developments
in Intergovernmental Relations
in Switzerland

Intergovernmental relations in flux – constitutional and other reforms
The issue of intergovernmental relations is not a question commonly
raised in Switzerland. However, it is still a question worth considering, as it
addresses all formal and informal aspects of life among the cantons and
with the Confederation. Swiss federal law has long used a "holistic" approach:
beyond the specific provisions, the machinery of legal institutions has
relied on civic common sense to hold the Confederation together.

Switzerland and its federation are characterized by:

- ☐ diversity (languages, religions, regions, etc.);
- ☐ smallness and small territorial entities (26 cantons and more than
  2700 communes);
- ☐ scarcity of resources;
- ☐ the need for cooperation;
- ☐ a paucity of raw materials;
- ☐ direct democracy;
- ☐ federalism and historically strong cantons.

The strength of the Swiss federal state stems not from a unique language, but from the common political will of the Swiss to live together.

Currently, Swiss federalism is in a state of flux. A great number of citizens are no longer bound to their cantons simply by virtue of their cultural affiliation and there is more emphasis on what is expected of government in the form of services. As well, new differences are arising, e.g. between urban, suburban and rural areas.

The cantons, and above all the Confederation (the federal government), have responded to these changes with substantial reforms, in particular with a total revision of the Federal Constitution (2000) and a comprehensive reform of the system of allocation of tasks and fiscal equalization (2008). This "country report 2009" intends primarily to discuss these reforms.

Intergovernmental relations in the service of the federal state – changes to a new system

1. In Switzerland, it is the people who mould the relationship between the Confederation and the cantons. The recent reforms have extended democracy – through more participation of the cantons, and wider consultations with the communes, or local government, and civil society.

2. In its role as a "federation", the federal state seeks a balance between diversity and unity. Traditionally, it provided for cultural diversity (language, etc.). Today, it also addresses both the evolution towards a more individualistic, more economically motivated society, and the need to deal with regional development differences.

3. In its role as a "state", the federal state must be able to fulfill common tasks better than the cantons would individually. The fulfilment of tasks is becoming more complex. The idea of these reforms is not simply a shift of individual tasks or a reallocation of funding, but a reorganization of the federal state and a modernization of federal forms of cooperation and partnership.

Intergovernmental relations as a means of reinforcing the federal state

The recent round of reforms is intended to give the Confederation, the cantons and in some cases the communes new redefined responsibilities.

The Confederation should concentrate on its strategic role. The cantons have more individual responsibility and bear more collective responsibility for the federal state, for which they are given a certain degree of financial adjustment.

The Constitution guarantees cantonal autonomy and puts it into specific terms in relation to the tasks that the cantons perform, and to their funding.

The reforms provide for an increased, two-tier separation of responsibilities and a new common set of rules for the implementation of the federal law through the cantons. The reforms also provide for increased participation by the cantons in the decision-making process of the Confederation, including more joint participation in the drafting of legislation.

The reforms also enunciate principles for the future allocation of tasks by the Constitution, or by other laws. Those principles are, for the most part, based on overarching principles of subsidiarity and fiscal equivalence.

In addition, the cantons now have more instruments to facilitate cooperation. In most cases, they are legally permitted to enter into agreements. And, with or without agreements, the Confederation and cantons cooperate intensively. There are new instruments like the "program agreements" on (strategic) programs and (operational) implementation, and the development of multi-tier cooperation and multi-level systems, as, for instance, in policies related to urban areas.

The reform of federalism can only be complete if the new allocation of tasks is complemented by financial reforms. The starting point is the financial autonomy of the cantons. They are (together with the communes) responsible for around 2/3 of public revenues and expenditure. However, the cantons' autonomy works only if each canton has sufficient financial latitude. The Confederation regulates the autonomy of the cantons in a number of ways: by a system for financial equalization, by a formal tax harmonization, and by requirements based on constitutional case law.

There is a new system of financial equalization, separate from the previous practice of subsidizing individual tasks. This new system consists of payments made by the Confederation and the "rich" cantons according to their potential tax revenues, and based on the costs of special structural burdens (such as the "geographic" costs of mountain regions and socio-demographic costs of the urban areas). As well this system is supplemented by a new type of federal subsidies to the cantons through (strategic) programs.

Obligation to cooperate and the resolution of disputes

Cooperation and financial equalization are supplemented by the obligation to share financial burdens among the cantons. If and when cooperation in the "sharing of burdens" fails, the federal Parliament (sometimes following a referendum) may impose an "obligation to contract", in individual cases.

In the new reforms the Swiss tradition of mutual respect and consensus is now expressly stated: disputes among cantons or between cantons and the Confederation are settled if possible by means of negotiations and mediation. The Confederation has the final say, but it must balance the interests of the Confederation and the interests of the individual cantons.

The example of European policy – challenges for intergovernmental relations

A special test for the Swiss federalism is European policy. The relationship with an evolving European Union has engendered many changes. In fact, since the 1990s, it has served as a driving force behind the reform of federalism. Foreign policy is now an express responsibility of the Confederation, but with three "federalist counterweights": the Confederation must pay heed to cantonal responsibilities and interests; the cantons may participate in "preparations" for decision-making at the federal level; and the cantons have the power to pursue their own special horizontal foreign policy, and in particular to enter into agreements. Meanwhile, cooperation with the EU has expanded to a series of over 120 agreements, with the result that it is possible to speak of Switzerland having an association-type relationship with the EU.

More active cooperation with the new-look EU has resulted in more limitations on the cantons than were originally expected. The Confederation has less latitude for giving due consideration to the cantons and must, increasingly, impose obligations on the cantons, while at the same time giving them less say in its decisions. However, the Confederation may not simply capitulate in the face of demands from the EU. The challenge lies in achieving compatibility with European policy and Swiss federalism.

> In the new reforms the Swiss tradition of mutual respect and consensus is now expressly stated: disputes among cantons or between cantons and the Confederation are settled if possible by means of negotiations and mediation. The Confederation has the final say, but it must balance the interests of the Confederation and the interests of the individual cantons.

The Swiss federal state is undergoing serious change in general. Whether the reforms will succeed is open to question. Whatever the case may be, further work is required to ensure the success of the reforms. To learn from other federal states is important.

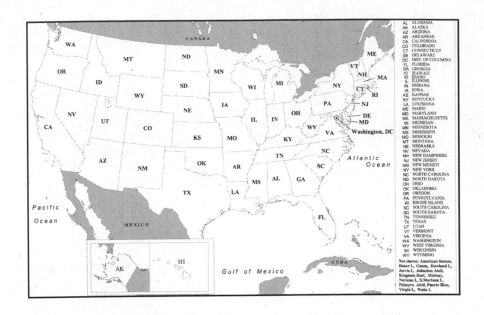

Intergovernmental Relations
in the United States of America:
Pervasive, Personal and Opportunistic

TROY E. SMITH

Unlike many new federal unions, the United States of America lacks formal structures or institutions to insure constituent units' powers and interests are represented and protected in the creation and administration of intergovernmental policies. America's founders did not perceive a need for such institutions, as federal and state governments were each given different responsibilities.

Today, intergovernmental relations pervade America's federal system. The federal government has involved itself in almost all aspects of domestic policy and, given the United States' large geographic size and population, the federal government requires constituent units' assistance to administer national policies.

While the national legislature, Congress, creates and the Executive implements the institutions and policies of the intergovernmental system, an informal intergovernmental system depends on personal relations among officials at all levels of government to coordinate and administer intergovernmental policies.

The growth of intergovernmental relations in the United States is due largely to demands for greater political action, in many sectors, and at all levels of government. The federal government has been particularly active in responding to many of these demands.

There are several reasons for this.

First, civic education has broken down and citizens no longer learn about their federal system and the different responsibilities of the state and local governments. Similarly, the rise of national media outlets, focusing on the national government, and the decline of local media coverage of state and local governments, have shifted public attention to the federal government. Consequently, citizens often identify their members of Congress, their federal representatives, as the ones to see regarding matters of public concern.

Federal elected officials, knowing their constituents expect action, are unwilling to tell their constituents to seek help from a different level of government.

Second, the institutions that once limited the national government's growth have eroded or been abolished.

> Today, intergovernmental relations pervade America's federal system. The federal government has involved itself in almost all aspects of domestic policy and, given the United States' large geographic size and population, the federal government requires constituent units' assistance to administer national policies.

Third, the states are often unable to effectively coalesce and work together to prevent the nationalization of policy.

Fourth, business interest groups often prefer a single national standard rather than different standards from each state, and interest groups may use the federal system to enlarge the scope of conflict to win their objectives.

Finally, many practitioners believe that the complexity of the global economy, trade and environmental problems require national or even international solutions.

The legislative branch, Congress, is the architect of the United States' intergovernmental system. Congress approves the legislation, and creates and oversees agencies to write regulations, disperse federal funds, and monitor constituent units' compliance with federal law and regulations.

Congress also affects constituent units' scope of action through monetary grants for specific activities, preemptions which prohibit constituent units from taking specific actions, and mandates which require constituent units to do certain things. Increasingly, members of Congress "earmark" funds for very specific projects because they distrust how agencies and constituent units will spend those funds.

In the last century, the Supreme Court removed many limits on federal powers. Despite efforts to restore some of those limits, only prohibitions against the federal government commandeering constituent units to administer federal policies and programs have prevailed. However, if a constituent unit accepts federal funds, it must abide by the federal rules attached to those funds.

Few states are able to constrain their appetite for federal funds. While the federal government increasingly funds its policies through public debt, 49 states are required to balance their budgets. Consequently, state and local governments often find it easier to seek and accept federal funds with attached requirements rather than find new revenue streams to fund favored policies.

Many informal structures that once fostered the representation and protection of constituent units' powers and interests have been lost or weakened. Before the 1970s, political parties fostered cooperation between federal and state officials and provided state officials a means to check the expansion of federal powers and policies. The adoption of direct primary elections (intra-party popular elections that select candidates for general elections) decreased state party officials' influence over members of Congress. Members of Congress now look not to their state party but to interest groups for the funding necessary to run (successful) campaigns.

Partisanship, nonetheless, has increased and impairs some intergovernmental relations. For example, national organizations representing state and local officials, such as the National Governors' Association (NGA), have often been unable to reach consensus on policy positions. Partisan organizations are more than willing to fill the void, and often issue competing and contradictory policy statements. Partisanship can also impair the personal relationships necessary for effective intergovernmental relations.

While the United State's Constitution and federal requirements guarantee citizens, and by extension the constituent units, a right to petition Congress and comment on proposed federal regulations, few constituent units take full advantage of these opportunities. Constituent units are most influential in the creation of federal policy when they coalesce and speak with a united voice, or when they have policy expertise to share.

The executive branch is responsible for the day-to-day running of intergovernmental policies and activities, and it relies on state and local governments to administer many of its policies. The size of the federal government's workforce has remained fairly constant for the last forty years, despite increases in the size of the American population, the increased complexity of American society and economy, and the growth of federal activities in domestic affairs. Over the same period, state and local governments, which administer much federal policy, have seen their workforces steadily increase.

Because of its often informal and unstructured nature, much of the management of intergovernmental relations in the United States depends on personal relationships among federal, state and local elected officials. The success of intergovernmental policy and program administration depends to a large degree on officials' developing and maintaining effective vertical and horizontal personal relationships. Yet, there is no training on how to navigate and negotiate intergovernmental relations. In fact, there are indications that connections among high-level officials in the different levels of government have declined significantly over time.

It seems that the development and maintenance of personal relations among organizations occur best when organization managers prioritize those relations for themselves and their staffs.

While some state and local intergovernmental obligations are enforceable through lawsuits, most federal agencies try to resolve differences outside of court through personal contacts or by withholding funds. Rarely are breaches of agreements taken to court. The courts are usually brought into a dispute by outside third parties.

How intergovernmental relations affect American democracy is unclear. Intergovernmental relations allow "multiple tracks" for citizens to access different levels of government, influence policy, and use one level to check or correct another level. Multiple tracks, however, favor interest groups with the resources to shift an issue to a different unit of government more favorable to them. Intergovernmental relations also obscure which unit or institution of government is responsible for a specific policy and, hence, hampers accountability. Intergovernmental relations appear to empower some and disempower others.

By shifting power to the national level, intergovernmental relations may diminish state and local government's responsiveness and ability to develop policies attuned to the diverse interests and objectives of the various constituents, communities and states that compose the United States.

America's system of intergovernmental relations has been called "opportunistic federalism" – all the actors in the system are opportunistic and use whatever arguments, instruments or tools help them accomplish their objective at the time. In this informal system, personal relationships are important to overcome impediments, navigate disagreements, and foster the level of collaboration and coordination necessary for effective policy making and administration.

Glossary

ASYMMETRY. Arrangements within a federation such that CONSTITUENT UNITS possess different status or powers.

AUTONOMOUS COMMUNITIES. The 17 territorial units of the Spanish state; created under the 1978 democratic constitution but not technically CONSTITUENT UNITS since their role and status has evolved through a process of devolution.

BENCHMARKING. Comparing performance between entities or organizations and learning from those exhibiting best practice.

BUNDESRAT. Second chamber of the German parliament, filled by appointed delegates of the LÄNDER governments; 'Federal Council'.

CANTONS. Title of the 26 CONSTITUENT UNITS of the Swiss Confederation.

COAG. (Council of Australian Governments) Peak intergovernmental meeting of the Prime Minister, the Premiers of the six STATES, Chief Ministers of the two self-governing TERRITORIES, and the President of the Australian Local Government Association.

COMMONWEALTH GOVERNMENT. The Australian government as distinct from the governments of the Australian STATES.

COMMUNES. Term for municipal governments in Switzerland.

CONCURRENT POWERS. Policy domains where the two levels of government in a federation are both granted constitutional authority or jurisdiction.

CONDITIONAL TRANSFERS. Intergovernmental grants with specific terms or conditions attached, requiring particular action to be taken by the recipient government within areas that are nominally the exclusive jurisdiction or authority of the recipient government; also 'tied grants'.

CONFEDERAL. A federal arrangement where sovereignty is retained by the CONSTITUENT UNITS and the central government has limited resources and exercises little independent authority (e.g. Swiss Confederation prior to 1848).

CONFERENCE OF PRESIDENTS. Meeting of the heads of government of the Spanish government and the governments of the AUTONOMOUS COMMUNITIES – all of which are PARLIAMENTARY in form, thus making this something of a misnomer.

CONSTITUENT UNITS.   The jurisdictions into which a federation is divided, enjoying constitutional status as partners in the union.

COORDINATION.   Intergovernmental practices whereby levels of government jointly develop and implement policies.

COOPERATIVE FEDERALISM.   Reality by which the clear division of powers and responsibilities in a classic 'dualist' federal system has given way to entanglement between the two levels of government and an extensive central government influence in areas of formerly and formally exclusive jurisdiction of the CONSTITUENT UNITS.

DELEGATED POWERS.   Jurisdiction exercised by a level of government on the authority of another level of government and revocable by that delegating government.

EARMARKING.   The practice of requiring specified grant funds to be spent by the recipient government on a specified purpose; see also CONDITIONAL TRANSFERS.

EUROPEAN COMMISSION.   The appointive body of the European Union that carries out the central governing function of the EU.

EXECUTIVE FEDERALISM.   Translation of the term used in Germany to describe a division of powers whereby the central government decides on policy but implementation and administration ('execution') are left to the CONSTITUENT UNITS (the LÄNDER); not to be confused with use of the term in the English-speaking world to describe the way relations between levels of government become concentrated at the executive level of government rather than the legislative.

FEDERAL COUNCIL.   (Bundesrat) The second chamber of the Austrian federation.

FEDERALISMO DE CONCERTACIÓN.   Term for cooperative federalism in Argentina.

FINANCIAL EQUALIZATION.   See HORIZONTAL FISCAL EQUALIZATION.

FISCAL EQUIVALANCE.   Principle that tasks should be assigned to the level of government whose boundaries most closely approximate to the footprint of the subject matter.

HIGH COURT.   The supreme court for constitutional and other law in the Australian federation; apex of the Australian judicial system.

HARMONIZATION.   The practice of making laws and regulations compatible between jurisdictions (without necessarily making them uniform).

HORIZONTAL COOPERATION.   Cooperation between governments of the CONSTITUENT UNITS of a federation independently of the central government.

HORIZONTAL FISCAL EQUALIZATION (HFE).   An arrangement for the redistribution of revenues within a federation to provide a minimum standard of resourcing across jurisdictions and thereby ensure citizens a comparable level of government services regardless of their place of residence. Typically based on a 'formula' that takes into account either or both the own-source revenue capacity and the expenditure requirements (needs) of the different jurisdictions.

INDIRECT FEDERAL ADMINISTRATION.   Austrian term for practice common to both German and Austrian federalism whereby the central government initiates policy or makes laws but responsibility for implementation and administration lies with the CONSTITUENT UNITS (LÄNDER); see also EXECUTIVE FEDERALISM.

INTER-STATE COMMISSION.   A body for regulating certain cross-jurisdictional matters mandated by the Australian Constitution but long defunct.

INTRASTATE FEDERALISM. Participation by the CONSTITUENT UNITS in the internal legislative process of the central government.

LÄNDER. Title of the CONSTITUENT UNITS of the German and Austrian federations; equivalent to States or provinces. Singular: *Land.*

LEVELS OF GOVERNMENT. Reference to the three orders of government in a federation: the LOCAL GOVERNMENTS, the CONSTITUENT UNITS, and the national government; also 'tiers'.

LOCAL GOVERNMENT. The 'third tier' of government, either urban municipalities (e.g. COMMUNES) or more rural counties, typically lacking constitutional status in a federation.

OPEN METHOD OF COORDINATION. The policy coordination technique used in the European Union in policy domains where the EU lacks jurisdiction and thus cannot employ directives; built around cooperative BENCHMARKING and inter-jurisdictional policy learning.

MINISTERPRÄSIDENTEN. The heads of government of the German *LÄNDER;* equivalent to premiers in Australian STATES or Canadian PROVINCES.

MINISTERIAL COUNCILS. Regular meetings between the Commonwealth ministers and their State counterparts in Australia in the various policy domains; work under auspices of COAG.

MIRROR LEGISLATION. Statutes passed in each jurisdiction using template from an originating jurisdiction so as to achieve HARMONIZATION.

NEO-LIBERAL REFORMS. Public policy reforms designed to allow much greater scope for market forces; notably privatisation, de-regulation, contracting out, fee-for-service.

ORDERS OF GOVERNMENT. See LEVELS OF GOVERNMENT.

PARLIAMENTARY SYSTEM. The version of representative democracy where the executive branch is elected from within the legislative branch and holds office for as long as it has the support of the elected legislature.

PROVINCES. Term for the CONSTITUENT UNITS of the federation in Argentina, Canada and South Africa.

RACE TO THE BOTTOM. Perceived tendency for policies – particularly in areas such as social welfare provision and environmental protection – to be driven down to a lower level by competitive pressures from other jurisdictions in a federation.

REFER POWERS. Possibility provided in the Australian Constitution for States, individually or collectively, to transfer policy responsibilities to the COMMONWEALTH GOVERNMENT, presumably on a revocable basis.

REVENUE SHARING. Formal arrangement, perhaps constitutionally entrenched, for LEVELS OF GOVERNMENT in a federation to share according to a set formula, revenues from a given source.

RESIDUAL POWERS. Authority or jurisdiction assigned to a level of government in a federation without those powers being specifically identified or enumerated and typically being formally limited only to the extent that the Constitution explicitly identifies areas not included.

RESPONSIBLE GOVERNMENT. The traditional term in the British colonial tradition for the principle of PARLIAMENTARY democracy that the political executive is formed in and answerable to the people's elected representatives in parliament.

SENATE. Name of the second chamber in various federations – including Argentina, Australia, Canada and the United States.

SPENDING POWER. The ability of central governments in federal systems to extend their policy influence into areas where the CONSTITUENT UNITS possess nominally exclusive jurisdiction by means of CONDITIONAL TRANSFERS; a corollary of VERTICAL FISCAL IMBALANCE.

STATE OF THE AUTONOMIES. Formal term for the Spanish constitutional order.

STATES. Term for the CONSTITUENT UNITS in various federations – including Australia, Brazil, India, Nigeria and USA.

STATUTES OF AUTONOMY. The constitutional charters of the AUTONOMOUS COMMUNITIES in Spain.

SUBSIDIARITY. Principle according to which responsibilities should be left to the lowest level of government that can perform them effectively; formula for the division of powers in the EU.

SUPREME COURT. The highest court for constitutional and other law in the Indian (and other) federation; apex of the Indian judicial system.

TERRITORIES. Australian jurisdictions lacking the constitutional status of CONSTITUENT UNITS, either self-governing through powers delegated by the COMMONWEALTH GOVERNMENT or directly administered.

UNION GOVERNMENT. Term for the central government of the Indian federation.

VERTICAL FISCAL IMBALANCE (VFI). An imbalance in revenues and responsibilities between the levels of government in a federation, with one level enjoying revenues in excess of its needs and the other or others bearing expenditure responsibilities in excess of their own-source revenues; also known as fiscal gap.

Contributors

MARC-ANTOINE ADAM, Director of Strategic Planning, Secrétariat aux affaires intergouvernementales canadiennes, Government of Québec, Canada

XAVIER ARBÓS MARÍN, Professor of constitutional law and dean of the Faculty of Law, University of Girona, Spain

MARTA ARRETCHE, Associate Professor, University of São Paulo and Research Director of the Center for Metropolitan Studies, Brazil

JOSÉE BERGERON, PH.D., Senior Advisor at the Strategic Planning Direction, Secrétariat aux affaires intergouvernementales canadiennes, Government of Québec, Canada

JULIA VON BLUMENTHAL, Professor of Political Science, Justus-Liebig-University Giessen, Germany

MARIANNE BONNARD, Senior Advisor at the Ministère des Relations internationales, Government of Québec, Canada

PETER BUßJÄGER, Director, Institute of Federalism, Austria

WALTER F. CARNOTA, Chair, Public Law, University of Buenos Aires, Argentina

MARÍA JESÚS GARCÍA MORALES, Professor, Constitutional Law, Autonomous University of Barcelona, Spain

NICOLAS LEVRAT, Professor, International Law, University of Geneva, Switzerland

ROLAND LHOTTA, Professor, Department of Political Science, Helmut Schmidt, Germany, Germany

EGHOSA E. OSAGHAE, Professor of Political Science and Vice Chancellor, Igbinedion University, Nigeria

M. P SINGH, Formerly Professor of Political Science at University of Delhi

DEREK POWELL, Director, Department of Provincial and Local Government, Republic of South Africa

THOMAS PFISTERER, Attorney at Law, Voser Rechtsanwälte, Switzerland

JOHN PHILLIMORE, Executive Director, John Curtin Institute of Public Policy, Curtin University of Technology, Australia

JOHANNE POIRIER, Professor and co-Director, Public Law Centre, Université Libre de Bruxelles, Belgium

REKHA SAXENA, Associate Professor, Department of Political Science, University of Delhi

CHERYL SAUNDERS, Personal chair in law, University of Melbourne, Australia, and President, International Association of Centres for Federal Studies

TROY E. SMITH, Associate Professor, Department of Political Science, Brigham Young University at Hawaii

Participating Experts

We gratefully acknowledge the input of the following experts who participated in the theme of Intergovernmental Relations in Federal Systems. While participants contributed their knowledge and experience, they are in no way responsible for the contents of this booklet.

Ursula Abderhalden, Universität St. Gallen, Switzerland
Fernando Abrucio, Instituto Universitário Europeo Fundação Getúlio Vargas, Brazil
Musa Abutudu, University of Benin, Nigeria
Ashraf Adam, Consultant, South Africa
Ralph Adeghe, Igbinedion University, Nigeria
Pedro Aguiló, Government of Balearic Islands, Spain
Eliseo Aja, University of Barcelona, Spain
Enoch Albertí, Universidad de Barcelona, Spain
Pere Almeda, Dep. Presidencia Generalitat Catalunya, Spain
V. N. Alok, Indian Institute of Public-Administration, Centre for Urban Governance, India
Esteban Rosa Alves, Ministry of Defense, Argentina
George Anderson, Forum of Federations, Canada
Xavier Arbós Marin, University of Girona, Spain
Balveer Arora, Centre for Political Studies, Jawaharlal Nehru University, India
Solomon Asemota, Ethnic Nationalities Movement, Nigeria
Sissi Auer, Insitute of Federalism, Austria
Andreas Auer, Zentrum für Demokratie Universität Zürich, Switzerland
Thorsten Augustin, Hanse-Office (Brüssel) Ministerium Justiz, Arbeit und Europa (Kiel), Germany
Bodo Bahr, Landtag Mecklenburg-Vorpommern, Germany
Gerald Baier, University of British Columbia, Canada
R. Balakrishnan, Election Commission of India, India
Jorge Bercholc, University of Buenos Aires, Argentina
Peter Berkowitz, European Commission, EU

Xavier Bernadí, Generalitat de Catalunya, Spain
Viviana Bonpland, Health Ministry, Argentina
Lorenz Bösch, Baudepartement, Switzerland
Linda Botterill, Australian National University, Australia
Canisius Braun, Universität St. Gallen, Switzerland
Eugénie Brouillet, Université Laval, Canada
Peter Brühwasser, Austrian League of Cities in Tyrol, Innsbruck, Austria
Marcelo Adrián Bufacchi, Cabinet Secretariat, Argentina
Peter Bußjäger, Insitute of Federalism, Austria
Werner Bussmann, Bundesamt für Justiz, Switzerland
Miguel Angel Cabellos, Universitat de Girona, Spain
Dominic Cardy, Forum of Federations, Canada
Walter F. Carnota, University of Buenos Aires, Argentina
Helena Castro, Unicamp, Brazil
Ricardo Ceneviva, Universidade de São Paulo, Brazil
Bidyut Chakrabarty, University of Delhi, Dept of Political Science, India
Rupak Chattopadhyay, Forum of Federations, India
Cesar Colino, Universidad Nacional de Educacíon a Distancia, Spain
Jordi Conde, Generalitat de Catalunya, Spain
Mercè Corretia, Universitat de Girona, Spain
Charles-Emmanuel Côté, Université Laval, Canada
Tom Courchene, Queen's University, Canada
Xavier de Pedro, Government of Aragon, Spain
Baron Philippe de Schoutheete, European Union, EU
Jaap De Visser, Community Law Centre, South Africa
Manfred Degen, Permanent representation of Germany to the EU, EU
Francisco del Rio, Junta de Andalucía, Spain
Frank Delmartino, Catholic University Leuven, EU
Ravi Dhingra, Inter-State Council Secretariat, Government of India, India
Norberto Di Battista Di Battista, Escuela de Abogados del Estado, Argentina
Isabelle Dirkx, European Union Committee of the Regions, EU
Jesús Divassón, Government of Aragon, Spain
Asita Djanani, Institute of Federalism, Austria
Nicolai Dose, Universität Siegen, Germany
V. K. Duggal, Commission on Centre-State Relations, India
Christopher Dunn, Memorial University, Political Science, Canada
Enaruna Edosa, University of Benin, Nigeria
Meredith Edwards, University of Canberra, Australia
Reiner Eichenberger, Universität Fribourg für Volkswirtschaftslehre, Switzerland
Annegret Eppler, Universität Tübingen, Germany
Rosa-F. Escrihuela, Universitat de Girona, Spain
Egbe Evbuomwan, Edo State House of Assembly, Nigeria
Freddy Evens, Flemish Foreign Affairs Council, EU

Hans Fahrländer, Aargauer Zeitung, Switzerland

Franz Fallend, Institute of Political Science, University of Salzburg, Austria

Hildegaard Fast, Western Cape Provincial Government, South Africa

Adam Fennessy, Department of Premier and Cabinet (Victoria), Australia

Helber Ferreira do Vale, Instituto Universitário Europeo Fundação Getúlio Vargas, Brazil

Yonatan Fessha, Community Law Centre, South Africa

Fabrice Filliez, Eidg. Departement für Auswärtige Angelegenheiten, Switzerland

Thomas Fischer, Bertelsmann Stiftung Office in Brussels, EU

Jean-René Fournier, Switzerland

Graziella Franzese, Secretariat of Provinces, Ministry of the Interior, Argentina

Cibele Franzese, Fundação Getúlio Vargas EAESP, Brazil

Joachim Fritz, GTZ, South Africa

Anna Gamper, Institute of Public Law, University of Innsbruck, Austria

Ángeles García Frías, Tribunal Constitucional, Spain

María Jesús García Morales, Autonomous University of Barcelona, Spain

Sol Garson, Universidade Federal do Rio de Janeiro, Brazil

Matthias Germann, Land Vorarlberg, Austria

Roger Gibbons, Canada West Foundation, Canada

Gerold Glantschnig, Government of the Land Kärnten, Austria

Robert Gmeiner, Austria

Wolfgang Göke, Niedersäch-Sischer Landtag, Germany

Sandra Gomes, Cem/ Cebrap, Brazil

Renata Gonçalves, SNH/ Mcidades, Brazil

Jimena Paula Gonzalez, Secretariat of Provinces, Ministry of the Interior, Argentina

Mireia Grau, Universitat de Girona, Spain

Diane Gray, Province of Manitoba, Canada

Martin Große-Hüttmann, Universität Tübingen, Germany

Anton Gstöttner, Land Tyrol, Austria

Fátima Guerreiro, Estado da Bahia, Brazil

Marcel Guignard, Schweiz. Städteverband, Switzerland

Maria Guimarães de, Unicamp, Brazil

Gabriel A. Gundu, Public Service Institute of Nigeria, Nigeria

Renuka Jain Gupta, Inter-State Council Secretariat, Government of India, India

Karen Harrison, Indigo, South Africa

Jeffrey Harwood, John Curtin Institute of Public Policy, Curtin University of Technology, Australia

Reinold Herber, Forum of Federations, Germany

Martin Huber, Association of the Municipalities, Salzburg, Austria

Andrea Iff, Universität Bern, Switzerland

Augustine Ikelegbe, University of Benin, Nigeria

Juded Ilo, Forum of Federations, Nigeria

Obajide Ilugbo, Igbinedion University Okada, Nigeria
Festus Imuetinyan, University of Benin, Nigeria
Karl Irresberger, Federal Chancellery, Vienna, Austria
Ade Isumonah, University of Ibadan, Nigeria
B. Jana, Inter-State Council Secretariat (ISCS), Government of India, India
Charlie Jefferey, ESRC Devolution and Constitutional Change Programme, University of Edinburgh, EU
Rajesh Jha, University of Delhi, Rajdhani College, India
Carolyn Johns, Ryerson University, Canada
Omorowa Jonah, ITV Benin, Nigeria
Mukul Joshi, Inter-State Council Secretariat, Government of India, India
Ferdinand Karlhofer, Institute of Political Science, University of Innsbruck, Austria
David Kemp, Australian and New Zealand School of Government, Australia
Sibonile Khoza, Premiers Office Western Cape Government, South Africa
Andreas Kiefer, Government of the Land Salzburg, Austria
Brad Kinsela, Department of Premier and Cabinet, Australia
Karl-Heinz Klär, Plenipotentiary of the Land of Rhineland-Palatinate to the Federal Government and for Europe, EU
Alberto Kleiman, Presidência da República , Brazil
Felix Knüpling, Forum of Federations, Germany
Arnold Koller, Forum of Federation, Switzerland
Christoph Konrath, Austrian Parliament, Vienna, Austria
Veena Kukreja, University of Delhi, Dept of Political Science, India
Krish Kumar, Ethekwini Metro, South Africa
Karl-Heinz Lambertz, Government of the German-speaking Community of Belgium, EU
Morris Lemma, New South Wales Parliament, Australia
Bernadette Leon, National Treasury, South Africa
Rudolf Lepers, Bundesmini-sterium für Wirtschaft u Technologie, Germany
Nicolas Levrat, University of Geneva, EU
Juan José López Burniol, Spain
Stefan Lütgenau, Indepedant Researcher, Austria
Naison Machingauta, Community Law Centre, South Africa
N. R. Madhava Menon, Commission on Centre-State Relations, India
K. Mahesh, Value Added Tax, India
Akhtar Majeed, Hamdard University, Centre for Federal Studies, India
Shiva Makotoko, ABSA Corporate and Business Bank, South Africa
Diana Mampel, Generalitat de Catalunya, Spain
Marco Mangini, Administración Federal de Ingresos Públicos, Argentina
Patricio Alejandro Maraniello, Fiscalía General Adjunta de la Ciudad Autónoma de Buenos Aires, Argentina
José Marí, Parliament of Comunidad Valenciana, Spain
Elena Marquesán, Government of Aragon, Spain

Gerard Martín Alonso, Universitat de Girona, Spain
Florence Masajuwa, Igbinedion University, Nigeria
Ken Matthews, National Water Commission, Australia
Annette May, Community Law Centre, South Africa
Roland Mayer, Konferenz der Kantonsregierungen, Switzerland
June McCue, University of British Columbia, Faculty of Law, Canada
Luzuko Mdunyelwa, City of Cape Town, South Africa
Ajay Mehra, Jamia Milia Islamia University, Centre for Dalit and Minorities Studies, India
Matthew Mendelsohn, University of Toronto, Canada
Jennifer Menzies, Council for Australian Federation, Australia
Johann Mettler, Salga, South Africa
Geraldine Mettler, Gauteng Government, South Africa
K. P. Mishra, Inter-State Council Secretariat, Government of India, India
Helena Mora Balcells, Universitat de Girona, Spain
Walter Moser, Konferenz der Kantonsregierungen, Switzerland
Amarjit Narang, Indira Gandhi National Open University, India
Dario Santiago Nassif, National Senate, Argentina
Alain Noël, Canada
Phindile Ntliziywana, Community Law Centre, South Africa
Amy Nugent, University of Toronto, Canada
Mary Ann O'Loughlin, Council of Australian Governments Reform, Australia
Theo Öhlinger, Institute of Constitutional Law and Administrative Law, University of Vienna, Austria
V.K. Ohri, India
Stephen Okhonmina, Igbinedion University Okada, Dept of Political Science, Nigeria
Peter Oliver, Faculty of Law, University of Ottawa, Canada
Godwin Onu, Nnamdi Azikiwe University, Nigeria
Ebere Onwudiwe, Central State University, Wilberforce, Ohio, Nigeria
Wendy Ovens, Wendy Ovens & Associates, South Africa
Babalola Owolabi, Oyo State Government, Nigeria
Sam Oyovbaire, TAS & Associates, Nigeria
Alexandre Padilha, Presidência da República, Brazil
Ian Peach, Office of the Federal Interlocutor for Metis and Non-Status Indians, Canada
Luigi Pedrazzini, Dipartimento delle Istituzioni, Switzerland
Benoît Pelletier, Université d'Ottawa, Canada
Jose Francisco Peña, Senado, Spain
Begoña Pérez de Eulate, Government of Basque Country, Spain
José María Pérez Medina, Spanish Premier Minister's Office, Spain
María del M. Pérez Velasco, Generalitat Catalunya, Spain
Peter Pernthaler, Institute of Public Law, University of Innsbruck, Austria
Irshad Perwez, Hamdard University, Centre for Federal Studies, India

Andrew Petter, Faculty of law, University of Victoria, Canada
Thomas Pfisterer, Attorney at Law, Rechtsanwälte, Switzerland
John Phillimore, John Curtin Institute of Public Policy, Curtin University of Technology, Australia
Leandro Piquet Carneiro, Universidade de São Paulo, Brazil
Andrew Podger, Institute of Public Administration Australia, Australia
Johanne Poirier, Université Libre de Bruxelles, Centre de Droit Public, EU
Derek Powell, Consultant, South Africa
Anne Racine, Secrétariat aux Affaires Intergouvernementales Canadiennes, Canada
Christian Ranacher, Office of the Land Government of Tyrol, Austria
Paula Ravanelli Losada, Presidência da República , Brazil
Antonio Revilla, Generalitat Catalunya, Spain
Fernando Rezende, Fundação Getúlio Vargas, Brazil
Gaetane Ricard Nihoul, Notre Europe, EU
Ramon Riu, Generalitat Catalunya, Spain
María José Rodríguez, Escuela de Abogados del Estado, Argentina
Héctor Rodríguez, Administración Federal de Ingresos Públicos, Argentina
Ignacio Sáez, Government of Castilla y León, Spain
Ana Florencia Salvatelli, Jefatura de Gabinete de Ministros de la Nación, Argentina
Patricio Sammartino, Procuración General de la Ciudad Autónoma de Buenos Aires, Argentina
Ignacio Sánchez, Parliament of Extremadura, Spain
Graham Sansom, University of Technology Sydney, Centre for Local Government, Australia
Júnia Santa Rosa, Secretaria Nacional de Habitaçáo, Ministério des Cidades, Brazil
Cheryl Saunders, University of Melbourne, Australia
Regine Sauter, Switzerland
David Savage, Consultant, South Africa
Rekha Saxena, Forum of Federations, India
Matthias Saxer, Neue Zürcher Zeitung, Switzerland
Dirk Schattschneider, Land Nordrhein-Westfalen, Germany
Valentina Schaumburger, Institute of Public Law, University of Innsbruck, Austria
John Schmidt, New South Wales Cabinet Office, Australia
Kai-Uwe Schnapp, Universität Hamburg, Fakultät für WiSo, Germany
Rainer J. Schweizer, Universität St. Gallen Büro FR-HSG, Switzerland
Leslie Seidle, Forum of Federations, Canada
Vijay Shankar, Commission on Centre-State Relations, India
Chanchal Sharma, Kurukshetra University, India
S. D. Sharma, Commission on Centre-State Relations, India
Sinazo Sibisi, Development Bank of Southern Africa, South Africa
Richard Simeon, University of Toronto, Canada

Julie Simmons, University of Guelph, Political Science, Canada
Ajay Kumar Singh, Hamdard University, Centre for Federal Studies, India
Dhirendra Singh, Commission on Centre-State Relations, India
Surendra Singh, Observer Research Foundation, Centre for Politics and Governance, India
M. P. Singh, Forum of Federations, India
Douglas Singiza, Community Law Centre, South Africa
Tanya Smith, Department of Premier and Cabinet, Australia
Mireia Soliellort, Government of Catalonia to the European Union, EU
Ágata Solernou, Generalitat de Catalunya, Spain
Niklas Sonntag, Institute of Public Law, University of Innsbruck, Austria
Norma Vicente Soutullo, Sindicatura General de la Nación, Argentina
Gerhard Stahl, European Union Committee of the Regions, EU
Valentina Staveris, Committee of the Regions, Forward Studies Unit, EU
Nico Steytler, Community Law Centre, South Africa
France St-Hilaire, Institute of Research on Public Policy, Canada
Kumar Suresh, Hamdard University, Centre for Federal Studies, India
Martina Suter, Universität Zürich, Switzerland
Béatrice Taulegne, European Union Committee of the Regions, EU
Adriana Tettamanti, Production and Economic Development Ministry, Province of San Juan, Argentina
Hendrik Theunissan, Committee of the Regions, Forward Studies Unit, EU
Erich Thies, Staatssekretär a.D. / General-sekretär der Kultusminister-konferenz, Germany
Erich Thöni, Institute of Political Finances, Austria
Veronika Tiefenthaler, Institute of Public Law, University of Innsbruck, Austria
Eva Tobola, Ministry of Finance, Vienna, Austria
José Trindade, Secretaria da Fazenda, Universidad Federal do Pará, Brazil
Hans Martin Tschudi, Furer & Karrer, Rechtsanwälte, Switzerland
Ben Turok, Parliament, South Africa
Anne Twomey, University of Sydney, Australia
Celestine Ukatu, Institute of Governance and Social Research, Nigeria
Horacio Vaccarezza, Director, Escuela de Abogados del Estado, Argentina
Carlos Hugo Valdez, University of Cordoba, Argentina
Santiago Valencia, Government of Galicia, Spain
Mirjam Van Donk, Isandla institute, South Africa
Philip Van Ryneveld, Hunter van Ryneveld, South Africa
Arnaud Van Waeyenberge, Université Libre de Bruxelles, EU
Bart Vanhercke, Observatoire Social Européen, EU
Peter Vaz, RTI International, South Africa
Nora Vignolo, Procuración General de la Nación, Argentina
Maite Vilalta, University of Barcelona, Spain
Silvia Villalonga, Fundación Ciudadanos Independientes, San Juan Province, Argentina

Joan Vintró, University of Barcelona, Spain
Carles Viver, Universitat de Girona, Spain
Julia Von Blumenthal, University of Giessen, EU
Bernhard Waldmann, Universität Fribourg Staats-und Verwaltungsrecht, Switzerland
Adam Wand, Office of Senator The Hon. Nick Sherry, Commonwealth Minister for Superannuation and Corporate Law, Australia
Michael Wisser, Wirtschafts-minister-konferenz, Germany
Franziska Zahn, Universität Gießen, Germany
Carolin Zwilling, Institute for Studies on Federalism and Regionalism, Bozen, Austria

Diversity and Unity in Federal Countries
Edited by César Colino and Luis Moreno
Senior Editor, John Kincaid

Published for the Forum of Federations and the International Association of Centers for Federal Studies (IACFS)
Global Dialogue on Federalism, Book Series, Volume 7

Examines the balance of diversity and unity in twelve federal or federal-type countries (Australia, Belgium, Brazil, Canada, Ethiopia, Germany, India, Nigeria, Russian, Spain, Switzerland and the United States of America). Leading scholars and practitioners illustrate the current political, socio-economic, spatial, and cultural diversity in their country before delving into the role that social, historical and political factors have had in shaping the present balance of diversity and unity. Authors assess the value that is placed on diversity by examining whether present institutional arrangements and public policies either restrict or enhance it, and address the future challenges of balancing diversity and unity in an increasingly populated and mobile world.

Authors include: Nicholas Aroney, Balveer Arora, Petra Bendel, Irina Busygina, César Colino, Frank Delmartino, Hugues Dumont, Marcus Faro de Castro, Assefa Fiseha, Thomas Fleiner, Alain-G. Gagnon, Mohammed Habib, Andreas Heinemann-Grüder, Maya Hertig Randall, John Kincaid, Gilberto Marcos Antonio Rodrigues, Luis Moreno, Richard Simeon, Roland Sturm, Rotimi T. Suberu, Sébastien Van Drooghenbroeck.

JOHN KINCAID is Professor of Government and Public Service and director of the Robert B. and Helen S. Meyner Center for the Study of State and Local Government at Lafayette College, Easton, Pennsylvania.
LUIS MORENO is a Research Professor at the Centre for Human and Social Sciences, Spanish National Research Council (CSIC), Spain.
CÉSAR COLINO is an Associate Professor at the Universidad Nacional de Educación a Distancia, Spain.

December 2008
6 x 9 12 maps

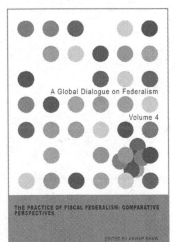

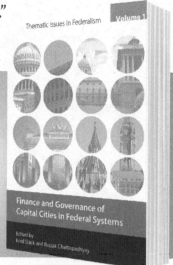

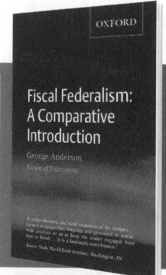

Federations: What's new in federalism worldwide

Edited by Rod Macdonell
Published three times per year

- A specialized magazine, geared toward practitioners of federalism, with stories on current events in federal countries and how these relate to their federal systems of government
- Theme-related articles that explore specific aspects of federal governance worldwide
- Each issue offers a snapshot of federalism in its current state around the world

I really enjoy reading the magazine. When I have finished reading an edition I have the sure sense that I am aware of the important events that are happening in most of the world's federations.

Arnold Koller, former
President of Switzerland

Send orders to

ORDER FORM: Fax to +1 (613) 244-3372

Please bill me (check one):

- ☐ $25 CDN per year in Canada
- ☐ €20 in euro zone
- ☐ $25 U.S. elsewhere

By: ☐ VISA   ☐ Mastercard

Credit Card number:_____

Expiry: _____/ _____/ _____

Signature: _____

Telephone/email: _____

Ship books to:_____

Name:_____

Organization:_____

Street:_____

City:_____

Prov./State:_____   Postal/Zip code:_____

Forum Publications / www.forumfed.org/en/products

Please send me

☐ Forumfed - electronic newsletter and email updates.   No charge

☐ Handbook of Federal Countries 2005   CA $65.00

☐ Dialogues on Constitutional Origins, Structure, and Change in Federal Countries.   CA $13.00

☐ Dialogues on Distribution of Powers and Responsibilities in Federal Countries.   CA $13.00

☐ Dialogues on Legislative, Executive, and Judicial Governance in Federal Countries. CA $13.00

☐ Dialogues on the Practice of Fiscal Federalism: Comparative Perspectives.   CA $13.00

☐ Dialogues on Foreign Relations in Federal Countries.   CA $13.00

☐ Dialogues on Local Government and Metropolitan Regions in Federal Countries.   CA $13.00

☐ Foreign Relations in Federal Countries.   CA $35.00

☐ Video: The Challenge of Diversity. /personal use for classroom   CA $20.00

     for educational broadcast.   CA $60.00

☐ Federalism in a Changing World.   CA $65.00

☐ The Art of Negotiation.   CA $25.00

Total: _____

Postage

North America: $5.00 CAD first book, $1.50 each additional.

Overseas: $5.50 CAD first book, $2.00 each additional)

Subtotal: _____

California/N.Y. State residents please add 8.25% sales tax: _____

Canadian residents please add 6% GST (GST number R132094343): _____

Total: _____

Payment

☐ Payment or credit card information must accompany order.

   Cheque/money order (Made payable to McGill-Queen's University Press).

☐ VISA   ☐ MasterCard

   Credit Card number:_____

   Expiry: _____/ _____/ _____

   Signature: _____

   Telephone/email: _____

   Ship books to:_____

   Name:_____

   Street:_____

   City:_____

   Prov./State:_____   Postal/Zip code:_____

Forum of Federations
THE GLOBAL NETWORK ON FEDERALISM

700-325 Dalhousie,
Ottawa ON K1N 7G2 Canada

Tel.: 613.244.3360
Fax.: 613.244.3372

Notes

Notes